Tanagers, Cardinals, and Finches
of the United States and Canada

Tanagers, Cardinals, and Finches of the United States and Canada

The Photographic Guide

David Beadle and J. D. Rising

Princeton University Press
Princeton and Oxford

Copyright © 2006 by Princeton University Press
Published by Princeton University Press, 41 William Street, Princeton, New Jersey 08540
In the United Kingdom: Princeton University Press, 3 Market Place, Woodstock, Oxfordshire
OX20 1SY
All Rights Reserved

Library of Congress Cataloging-in-Publication Data

Beadle, David, 1961–
Tanagers, cardinals, and finches of the United States and Canada :
the photographic guide / David Beadle and J.D. Rising.
    p.   cm.
Includes bibliographical references.
ISBN-13: 978-0-691-11858-1 (pbk. : alk. paper)
ISBN-10: 0-691-11858-2 (pbk. : alk. paper)
1. Tangers—North America—Identification.   2. Cardinals (Birds)—North America—
Identification.   3. Finches—North America—Identification.   I. Rising, Jim.   II. Title.
QL696.P282B43   2006
598.8'75'097—dc22
2005048823

British Library Cataloging-in-Publication Data is available

This book has been composed in Stone Serif with Gill Sans Family Display

Printed on acid-free paper. ∞

pup.nathist.princeton.edu

Printed in Italy by Eurografica

1 3 5 7 9 10 8 6 4 2

DB would like to dedicate this book
to the memory of Bev Collier.

JR dedicates this book to
Justus, Nigel, and Fintan Rising, with love.

Contents

List of Species Covered

Acknowledgments

We are indebted to many people who shared with us their knowledge of North American tanagers, cardinals, buntings, and finches. Among those most helpful were Curtis Adkisson (Red Crossbills and Pine Grosbeaks), Craig Benkman (crossbills), Julie Craves (American status of European Goldfinches), Ron Martin (North Dakota), Ken and Mary Lou Schneider (rosy-finches), and Declan Troy (redpolls). The manuscript benefited greatly from the many constructive comments given by Trudy Rising and Linda Stanyer. Kimball Garrett and Brian L. Sullivan provided careful and helpful reviews of the first draft of the manuscript. Mark Peck and Glen Murphy of the Royal Ontario Museum kindly arranged access to its research collections for David Beadle. David Agro kindly provided much assistance with the scanning of several images for the book. Paul Prior and Dan Derebyshire gave expert opinions on tricky aging and sexing issues regarding some of the images that appear in the book. John Quaggin and Peter Thomas provided sonic assistance that was deemed essential to the completion of the task. We also greatly appreciate the close cooperation and patience shown by the many photographers who contributed to this book.

As well, we are indebted to Robert Kirk of Princeton University Press, who has encouraged us in every stage of this book's development. Finally, we are indebted to our families, especially to Trudy Rising, Katie Thomas, and James Beadle, who have continued to be both patient and fully supportive. Thanks to you all!

Introduction

This photographic guide to the North American tanagers (including the Bananaquit), cardinal grosbeaks, and finches aims to illustrate with clear photographs and detailed descriptions each of the forty-six species that have been recorded in the United States and Canada (biogeographically, most of Mexico is in North America, but we do not cover Mexican species other than those that also occur north of there). We also illustrate as many different plumages of these species as space and the availability of photos permit. Some of the species covered show geographic variation (that is, individuals from different parts of the range differ in appearance); biologists have often named different populations of geographically variable species as different *subspecies* (for more on subspecies, see **geographic variation** under "Organization of the Guide," below).

Although space—and, again, availability of good photographs—do not permit us to illustrate all of the variation within species or all of the named subspecies (many of which are only slightly differentiated), we have selected photographs to show as much of the range of variation within each species as we can.

General Identification Problems

A number of general identification problems are encountered by birders and biologists in the field such as judging size, coloration (because of variation in lighting), and the effects of age and seasonal variation in appearance. As well, for many species, it is often difficult to get a good look at the bird. To help deal with these problems, an observer in the field should ask a number of questions when confronted with an identification problem.

(1) How large is the bird? Generally, it is not possible to measure the individual in the field, but usually there will be some other object near the bird that can serve as comparison, perhaps another bird of known identity. If you are comparing the unknown bird with other birds, is it larger or smaller than the other birds present? With experience, it becomes possible to assess fairly accurately the size of the bird even if the environment gives few cues. Thus, with practice, you say that a Blue Grosbeak is simply too large to be an Indigo Bunting (of course, there are other important differences to look for).

(2) What are its markings? Although many of the species covered in this book are more or less unicolored (e.g., Indigo Buntings, Summer Tanagers, and Northern Cardinals), others have fairly complex patterning (e.g., the Bananaquit or male goldfinches). When in the field, try to note as much of this as you can. Also note the colors of bare parts: Are the feet and legs pink or dark? Is the bill red? And so forth.

(3) How does the bird act? Is its flight direct like that of a Scarlet Tanager or undulating like that of a goldfinch? Does it wag or "pump" its tail? Does it perch openly or in a hidden place? When on the ground, does it walk, hop, or shuffle? Is it in a flock? (Finches are commonly found in flocks outside the breeding season.)

(4) How about its ecology? Many species are characteristically found in coniferous

or mixed woods (e.g., crossbills and siskins); others are usually found in deciduous woods or thickets (e.g., tanagers and buntings). Dickcissels are found in weedy fields and along roadsides, and many buntings and finches commonly appear at feeders. Ask yourself: Is this the kind of place where you would expect to see the species you suspect you may be observing—is it in the appropriate habitat and within the species' range? For example, if you see a bird singing from the top of a spruce tree, it almost certainly is not a Dickcissel. If it is singing from the top of a weed in a field, it is probably not an Evening Grosbeak.

(5) When in the field, take careful note of the bird's behavior, general size, and shape. Does it appear to be long legged? How long is the tail relative to the body size? What is its shape? If you see the bird well, check its primary projection—that is, how far the longest primary projects beyond the tip of the longest tertial (a general measure of how long and pointed a wing is)—although this probably is not an important character for most of the species covered in this book. How far does the tail extend beyond the tip of the wing? Note the bill shape, often a critical indicator of what group of birds an individual is in. Bill shape is diagnostic for some species (e.g., Pyrrhuloxia). If you have the bird in hand, note its wing formula (the lengths of the primaries relative to each other). Also, if you can, take note of the shape of the primaries and rectrices; this is often a good indicator of age. It is often far more effective to write a quick note about the striking features of the bird and its behavior than to flip through your guides trying to find a picture similar to the bird you are observing. If you are with another person, quietly exchange observations. The other person may have noted something that escaped your attention. Concentrate on getting as good a look at the bird as possible, and consult the books later!

(6) What sounds does the bird make? Take careful note of its vocalization, including the call notes, which often significantly aid in identification.

(7) Lastly, what seems wrong about a tentative identification? Be especially careful about identifying a bird that appears to be out of range, in atypical habitat, or present at the wrong season, especially if you do not have previous experience with the species. Also remember that some birds are simply aberrant. For example, some Red Crossbills have white wing bars, whereas most do not.

The American Ornithologists' Union (AOU) *Check-list of North American Birds* (7th edition, 1998) places several groups of songbirds that have nine primary wing feathers in different families (the family is a category in standard zoological classifications). Other authorities recognize these same groups but often call them subfamilies of a larger, more inclusive family. Following the current AOU *Check-list*, the families are the New World wood-warblers (family Parulidae), the Bananaquit (Coerebidae), the tanagers (Thraupidae), the cardinal grosbeaks (Cardinalidae), the buntings and New World sparrows (Emberizidae), and the New World blackbirds (Icteridae). These families are all closely related, and the correct placement of many species in these families is not clear. For example, the Bananaquit is probably in the family Thraupidae, so it will soon be taken out of the Coerebidae (because the Bananaquit is the only species in that family, the Coerebidae will disappear), and the tanagers in the genus *Piranga* (e.g., the Scarlet, Summer, Hepatic, and Western tanagers) are probably best placed in the Cardinalidae. With the exception of the Emberizidae, a family that is widespread in the Old World, these families of birds occur only in the New World. An additional family, the Fringillidae, includes the finches, including the Pine and Evening grosbeaks, siskins, redpolls, finches, and crossbills. These birds are widespread in both the Old and New worlds, and according to molecular evidence they are not so closely related to the families listed above as those families are to each other. In this book we have limited our coverage to the Bananaquit, tanagers, cardinals, and finches that occur in the United States and Canada. We have treated the North American Emberizidae in other books, and there are excellent books on the warblers (Curson et al., 1994, and Dunn and Garrett, 1997) and the blackbirds (Jaramillo and Burke, 1999).

Overview of the Genera Covered in This Book

Within a family, several different genera (plural of genus) often are grouped together. It is conventional to italicize generic names. Thus the Red Crossbill is in the genus *Loxia*. It is also conventional to italicize the "scientific" (Latin) name of each species: the Red Crossbill is *Loxia curvirostra*. The White-winged Crossbill is closely related to the Red Crossbill, and therefore it is put in the same genus; its scientific name is *Loxia leucoptera*. The House Finch is less closely related to the Red Crossbill than it is to some other finches, and it is put in a different genus, *Carpodacus*, along with several other species that are closely related to it. These birds, because they are all fairly closely related to one another, are all put in the same family, Fringillidae. The Northern Cardinal is less closely related and is placed in a different family, Cardinalidae. These scientific names are internationally recognized, and the Latin name does tell us something about relationships (closely related species are put in the same genus, at least). Most of us use English vernacular names when talking about these birds, but these vernacular names can be misleading about evolutionary affinities. Early English-speaking settlers and biologists in the New World often named North American birds after European birds that appeared to be similar. Thus the name "grosbeak" is given to some songbirds with large, finch-like beaks, such as the Pine Grosbeak of Eurasia (and North America). However, the Pine and Evening grosbeaks are finches (Fringillidae), whereas the Rose-breasted, Black-headed, and Blue grosbeaks—also birds with large finch-like bills—are in the family Cardinalidae; that is, they are not particularly closely related to the other ("true") grosbeaks. Similarly, the British refer to species in the family Emberizidae as "buntings." Our Snow Bunting, also found in the Old World, is indeed a bunting in the "Old World" sense, as is the Lark Bunting, but the other American buntings (e.g., Indigo, Lazuli, Varied, and Painted buntings) are closely related to the cardinals. Recently published information on the molecular similarities among some of these nine-primaried songbirds show that the tanagers that are common in North America (in the genus *Piranga*) are best placed with the cardinals (not the tanagers), although they retain the well-established name "tanager" in their English name. Thus the Scarlet Tanager is still called the Scarlet Tanager, even though it is more closely related to the cardinals than to the true tanagers. So, as you can see, names may be deceptive.

The following is a list of the genera covered in this book, with a few comments about their characteristics and classification:

Genus Coereba (species no. 1).

This is a monotypic genus (i.e., there is only one species in the genus) that includes only the Bananaquit, a small songbird with a rather slim, decurved bill. Historically, this species has been placed in the monotypic family Coerebidae (this family formerly contained the other thin-billed tanagers—the honeycreepers and *Dacnis*), but molecular studies show that Bananaquits are probably tanagers (family Thraupidae); their closest relatives may be the *Tiaris* grassquits (which are often classified as New World sparrows) and the Galapagos ("Darwin's") finches. Bananaquits are common in the West Indies (except Cuba) and from central Mexico south to central South America. They occur irregularly in southern Florida.

Genus *Piranga* (species nos. 2–6).

Piranga are medium-sized songbirds with relatively stout but not conical bills. They are sexually dimorphic in color, and the males are brightly colored. Historically, they have been classified as tanagers (family Thraupidae), which morphologically they appear to be, but molecular studies clearly show that they are not tanagers but are probably in the family that contains the cardinals, *Pheucticus* grosbeaks, and *Passerina* buntings. Nonetheless, the name "tanager" is retained in their English names (e.g., Scarlet Tanager).

Genus *Spindalis* (species no. 7).

Spindalis were formerly known as "stripe-headed tanagers," and they recently have been split into four different species, all of which occur in the Bahamas and Greater Antilles. The Western Spindalis, which breeds in the Bahamas and Cuba, occasionally wanders to Florida. Molecular studies show that *Spindalis* are not tanagers, but it is not clear at this time in which family they are best placed.

Genus *Thraupis* (species no. 8).

Thraupis are fairly large tanagers of the Neotropics. Although the genus does not contain many species, some are among the most conspicuous of the tanagers and occur in towns and even sometimes in large cities. They have squeaky voices and characteristically are not found in deep forests. The only *Thraupis* in our area is introduced but at present is not established. *Thraupis*, apparently, really are tanagers.

Genus *Cyanerpes* (species no. 9).

The *Cyanerpes* honeycreepers are small, colorful, sexually dimorphic tanagers with thin, downcurved bills. They were formerly placed in the Coerebidae, which they resemble, but they apparently are tanagers (or perhaps in the Emberizidae), perhaps closely related to *Dacnis*.

Genus *Rhodothraupis* (species no. 10).

The Crimson-collared Grosbeak, which is casual in our area, is the only species in the genus *Rhodothraupis*. These are fairly large songbirds, related to the cardinals and *Pheucticus* grosbeaks; they have a relatively long tail, short wings, and a distinctly curved culmen, and are sexually dimorphic in plumage.

Genus *Cardinalis* (species nos. 11–12).

Two of the three species in the genus *Cardinalis* breed in the area covered in this book, and the Northern Cardinal occurs north into southern Canada. The third, the Vermillion Cardinal, is found in arid areas on the Caribbean coast of South America. The cardinals are long tailed, crested, and stout billed, and are sexually dimorphic in color.

Genus *Pheucticus* (species nos. 13–15).

The *Pheucticus* grosbeaks are stout-billed grosbeaks with rather short tails. They are sexually dimorphic in color, and the males are brightly colored. Three of the four species in *Pheucticus* occur in our area, but one of these, the Yellow Grosbeak, is only casual north of Mexico.

Genus *Cyanocompsa* (species no. 16).

Cyanocompsa grosbeaks or buntings are medium-sized finches; males are bright blue, whereas females are brown. Only one species, the Blue Bunting, occurs in our area, and it is casual in southern Texas and Louisiana.

Genus *Passerina* (species nos. 17–21).

Of the six species of *Passerina* buntings, four breed north of Mexico. They are small finches that are sexually dimorphic in color. Although the females are rather nondescript brown or green birds, the males are all brightly colored. They have a characteristic tail-"switching" behavior.

Genus *Spiza* (species no. 22).

Spiza is a monotypic genus, containing only the Dickcissel, a sparrow-like bunting that is locally abundant in the Midwest. The evolutionary affinities of *Spiza* are uncertain. They may be in the family of New World blackbirds (Icteridae) or aberrant cardinals (Cardinalidae); in most current classifications they are put in the Cardinalidae.

Genus *Fringilla* (species nos. 23–24).

The three species of *Fringilla* are generally placed in a separate subfamily (Fringillinae) in the family Fringillidae (the other finches are placed in the Carduelinae). *Fringilla* are robust finches that walk with a characteristic shuffling, jerky gait and have an undulating, bounding flight. The Brambling is a regular migrant through the western Aleutian Islands, Alaska, but the Chaffinch is casual in North America.

Genus *Leucosticte* (species nos. 25–27).

The three North American species of rosy-finches, or leucostictes, were formerly classified as one geographically variable species—indeed, some experts consider these to be races of a single Holarctic species, *Leucosticte arctoa*, the Arctic Rosy-Finch. They are dark sparrow-like finches that live mostly in alpine or high-altitude habitats, although in the far north Gray-crowned Rosy-Finches are found in barren, rocky areas at lower elevations, especially on islands.

Genus *Pinicola* (species no. 28).

There are only two species in the genus *Pinicola*, the Holarctic Pine Grosbeak and the Red-headed Rosefinch, which lives in the Himalayas, Tibet, and China. They are robust finches with relatively long tails and short, curved bills. They appear to be closely related to the crossbills and *Carpodacus* finches.

Genus *Carpodacus* (species nos. 29–32).

There are twenty-three species of *Carpodacus*, of which three are common in North America and a fourth is vagrant. They are medium-size finches with stout bills; adult males generally are red or rose colored, whereas females are brown and streaked—reminding one of sparrows.

Genus *Loxia* (species nos. 33–34).

The bills of crossbills (*Loxia*) are highly specialized to extract seeds from conifer cones, thus clearly separating crossbills from all other birds. At present, we recognize two species from North America, although the Red Crossbill is highly variable. Among the Red Crossbills there are several distinct song and call types, and it has been suggested that several different species of them exist.

Genus *Carduelis* (species nos. 35–43).

The North American *Carduelis*—the redpolls, siskins, and goldfinches—are all fairly small finches, but the greenfinches of Eurasia are larger (the Oriental Greenfinch is a vagrant in the Aleutian Islands, Alaska). The goldfinches are among the few finches to have two nearly complete molts per year, and thus distinctive summer and winter plumages. *Carduelis* are often found in mixed flocks of finches—especially with other *Carduelis*—and commonly come to feeders.

Genus *Pyrrhula* (species no. 44).

Pyrrhula, or bullfinches, are fairly large, colorful birds, with short, stubby bills that are adapted to feeding on buds. They are Eurasian birds, but the Eurasian Bullfinch is casual in Alaska. The subspecies that wanders to Alaska breeds in northeastern Asia and closely resembles the bullfinches of western Europe.

Genus *Coccothraustes* (species nos. 45–46).

The *Coccothraustes* grosbeaks are large, large-billed, stocky finches. The Hawfinch of Eurasia is casual in western Alaska. The two American species (one, the Hooded Grosbeak, occurs only in the cloud forests of Central America and Mexico; the other is the Evening Grosbeak) are often put into genus *Hesperiphona*.

Organization of the Guide

The main section of the guide consists, of course, of the species accounts of all species in the selected groups that occur in the New World north of Mexico. These are arranged in the sequence of the AOU *Check-list* (7th edition, 1998) and supplements to that *Check-list* published annually. This sequence is slightly different from that in the guides currently available, most of which were based on earlier editions of the *Check-list*.

Each account begins with **measurements** (total body length and wing length in both metric and English units, and mass in grams). The measurements are from Ridgway (1901) or other sources cited at the end of the account. The data on mass are from either Dunning (1993) or other sources cited in the accounts.

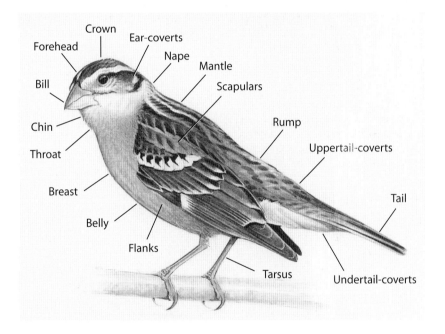

A brief statement is then provided about the species and its important features that aid in identification. A summary of the species' **habitat** preferences, characteristic **behavior,** and **voice** follows. We then describe **similar species** and summarize the species' **geographic variation**. We mention named subspecies if they occur north of Mexico and note general trends of variation. For the most part, geographic variation is clinal; that is to say, there are gradual geographic trends in features such as color and size. In the past, ornithologists commonly "chopped up" these clines, describing different parts of them as different subspecies. *A subspecies is a geographically and morphologically defined population (or group of populations) of a species.* Individuals from different subspecies of the same species are presumably interfertile; if they were known to be otherwise, they would be named as different species. Subspecies are given

Adult male Dickcissel

First-winter female White-winged Crossbill

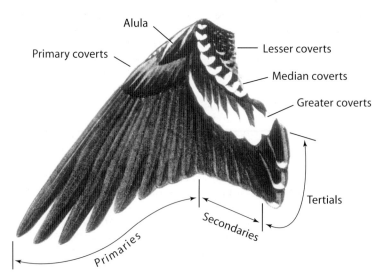

a three-part name; the first two parts are the same as the specific name. Thus *Carduelis flammea flammea* and *Carduelis flammea rostrata* are both subspecies of the Common Redpoll (*Carduelis flammea*). When portions of clines are named as different subspecies, geographically adjacent subspecies usually grade into one another, and therefore *it often is not possible to identify each individual as to subspecies*. It is important to emphasize that each subspecies has a specific breeding range. Thus, a nonbreeding bird that is migrating or on its wintering grounds cannot be positively identified to the subspecies level, although if the subspecies is well marked, individuals can be identified to subspecies outside the breeding season with a high degree of probability. Also, it is important to note that essentially *all* of the individuals breeding in the range of a named subspecies, unless they are on the edge of that range, are members of that subspecies *by definition*. Thus, a Common Redpoll breeding in Alaska is by definition in the subspecies *Carduelis flammea flammea* (often written simply *Carduelis f. flammea*). The variability among individuals breeding in the range of a subspecies defines the variability in that subspecies.

Following the discussion of geographic variation, we give a brief summary of the species' **distribution**, then discuss its **conservation status**. This is followed by a description of the species' **molts** and a rather detailed **description** of its appearance. Lastly, there is a summary of records of **hybrids** followed by a list of the principal **references** consulted for the account.

Age Terminology

We follow Humphrey and Parkes's (1959) terminology for plumages and molts, which, in sequence, is as follows: **Natal down, Prejuvenal molt, Juvenal plumage, First Prebasic (or Prebasic I) molt, First Basic or (Basic I) plumage, First Prealternate (Prealternate I) molt, First Alternate (Alternate I) plumage, Definitive Prebasic molt, Definitive Basic plumage**, and so on. Molts may be complete (involving all the feathers, but, of course, not all feathers are lost at the same time) or partial. For most North American songbirds, the Prejuvenal molt is complete, and it takes place before the young leave the nest. The First Prebasic molt may be partial or complete, and it takes place in the late summer or fall (commonly, but not always, before migration). Thus, the bird winters in Basic plumage (in the first year, this is the First Basic plumage). Commonly in American songbirds there are no Prealternate molts, but if they occur they are generally partial. Songbirds breed in either Basic or Alternate plumage, depending on whether or not they have a Prealternate molt. Some species have an additional molt, a **Presupplemental molt** that takes place before the Prebasic molt.

We use the term **nestling** to refer to a bird in the nest, **juvenile** to refer to a bird in Juvenal plumage, and, generally, **adult** to refer to a bird in Alternate or Definitive Basic plumage. In some species, such as the crossbills, it is possible to differentiate in the field birds of different ages, in which case we refer to them as **first fall** or **first winter**, etc; a **first-summer** bird is one that was born the previous summer and thus is approximately one year old. In *Carpodacus* some or all first-year males resemble females, but the first-year males of most species can be distinguished from females.

Range Maps

A range map is provided for each species covered in this book that breeds within the United States and Canada. A typical range map is shown below.

■ Breeding
▨ Year-round
■ Winter

Map colors

Red: Areas where the species may be found nesting in suitable habitat.
Green: Areas where the species may be found throughout the year.
Blue: Areas where the species may be found more or less regularly in winter.

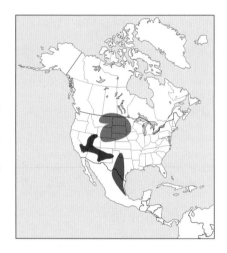

The colored areas show the usual distribution of the species (places where it is reported each year). The text (**distribution** section) should be consulted for more detailed information on each species' distribution, especially for places where the species occurs only occasionally or as a vagrant, or if annually, only rarely. For many migratory species, there are comments in this section on their usual migratory routes. Although migrants may turn up anywhere, each species is generally found only in a specific preferred habitat. For example, crossbills are usually found only in coniferous woods and, in summer, Dickcissels in tallgrass lands.

ı Bananaquit

(Coereba flaveola)

Measurements
Length: 10–12 cm; 4–5 in. (males slightly larger than females).
Wing: 50–60 mm; 2–2.4 in.
Mass: 7.4–12.5 g, av. 9.4 g (Puerto Rico).

Bananaquits are small, colorful Neotropical songbirds. They have a sharp, slightly decurved bill, a conspicuous white superciliary stripe, white throat and undertail coverts, yellow belly, dark postocular stripe, crown, and back, with a yellow rump. There is white in the base of the primaries and in the corners of the outer rectrices. They have a distinctive red gape.

Habitat   Bananaquits can be found in a wide variety of habitats, and within their range are absent only from very dry areas or high mountains. Commonly, they are found near flowering plants. They are common in gardens, clearings, and plantations, and in parts of their range also mangroves and dense humid forests. They occur from sea level to 1500 m.

Behavior   Their slender, pointed, and slightly decurved bills are used for piercing the bases of flowers to obtain nectar, their principal food, which they also obtain by clinging to plants and probing into flowers. Bananaquits also eat a variety of arthropods and some seeds. They sing persistently throughout the day and year.

Voice   The song is geographically variable. In the Bahamas, it is a series of buzzy ticks or hisses followed by a rapid, thin insect-like clicking. The call note is a warbler-like *tsip, seep,* or *sint*; it is similar to the call of the Hermit Thrush.

Similar species   The Bananaquit is a distinctive small bird with a thin bill; it looks like a warbler or vireo but has a short, square tail. Immatures can suggest a female Black-throated Blue Warbler, but the warbler does not have the red gape mark of the Bananaquit.

Geographic variation   There is a great deal of geographic variation in Bananaquits, with thirty-five to forty-one races recognized in various lists. However, all verifiable records from North America are of white-throated birds and probably represent the Bahamian subspecies (*C. f. bahamensis*), which is the subspecies described here, although some could be from the Yucatán Peninsula.

Distribution   *Resident* on most West Indian islands (but absent from Cuba) and in Mexico from s Veracruz and Oaxaca to n Chiapas and Guatemala, Belize, locally along the coast of Quintana Roo (including Cozumel Island), in the Caribbean lowlands of Honduras and Nicaragua, on both slopes of Costa Rica (absent in nw) and Panama, and south into South America south to nw Peru, central Bolivia, Paraguay, and extreme n Argentina. Irregular and rare winter visitor to Florida (August, November–May); most records from the Keys and southern peninsula but reported n to Pinellas, Polk, and Orange counties.

Conservation status   This is a widespread, common, and adaptable species, and in many places is the commonest small songbird. The Bananaquit commonly occurs near people and their gardens.

Molt   In Panama molt occurs in February and March.

Description   **Adults** (sexes similar)—Small, with thin, downcurved bill. *Head*, crown, lores, and postocular stripe blackish, supercilium white, and gape red; *back* blackish; *rump* yellow; *wing* blackish, with white bases to the primaries; underwing coverts white; *tail* short and square, with light tips to the outermost rectrices; *underparts*, throat, vent, and undertail coverts white, belly yellow; *bill* blackish or dark gray; *legs* and *feet* dark gray, claws black; *iris* dark brown. **Juveniles**—Similar to adults but grayish rather than dark gray and black; yellow belly less bright.

Hybrids   None reported.

References   Raffaele et al. (1998), Skutch (1954), Wetmore et al. (1984).

1.1 Bananaquit *Coereba flaveola bahamensis*, Abaco, Bahamas, February 1998. Small and warbler-like in appearance with short, decurved bill. Dark dusky brown upperparts with contrasting broad white supercilium and small white patch at base of primaries. Underparts white, with yellow patch on lower breast and belly. Note bright red base to lower mandible. This form is endemic to the Bahamas and is a rare vagrant to Florida (Kevin T. Karlson).

2 Hepatic Tanager

(Piranga flava)

Measurements
Length: 19.0–20.5 cm; 7.5–8.0 in.
Wing: 93–109 mm; 3.7–4.3 in. (sexes similar in size).
Mass: 23.2–47.4 g, av. 38.0 g (Mexico).

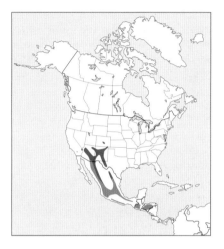

Although the Hepatic Tanager in our area is limited to the Southwest, overall it is the most widespread of the *Piranga* tanagers (it is widespread in Central and South America, south to Argentina). *Piranga* is the only genus of tanagers (if, indeed, they are tanagers—see introduction) that occurs in the United States and Canada. Adult male Hepatic Tanagers are orange red in color (liver colored, hence "hepatic"), whereas females are yellowish (the Latin name *flava* reminds us of that). Although the Hepatic Tanager is currently considered a single geographically variable species, molecular genetic data suggest that there indeed may be up to three species: the Hepatic Tanager (*Piranga hepatica*) of the southwestern United States south to Nicaragua, the "Tooth-billed" Tanager (*P. lutea*) of Costa Rica to northern and western South America, and the "Red" Tanager (*P. flava*) of eastern and southeastern South America.

Habitat The Hepatic Tanagers of the United States are found in open montane pine-oak forests, often (in summer) with little ground cover. In migration they are occasionally seen in lowland woods, sometimes feeding in groups on the ground. The few that winter in California are usually found in planted pines.

Behavior When feeding, their movements are slow and deliberate. In migrating and wintering groups, they may forage in flocks of mixed-species composition including warblers, orioles, and other tanagers; some attend army-ant swarms.

Voice The Hepatic Tanager's song is a rich, rambling series of five to seven elements, with each phrase separated by distinct pauses. The songs of Summer Tanagers or Black-headed Grosbeaks are somewhat similar, but more continuous. The Summer Tanager song lacks the buzzy or harsh quality of the song of Scarlet Tanagers. The call is an abrupt *tchup* or *chuck*. In flight they also give a quiet *weenk* note.

Similar species Hepatic Tanagers of all ages and sexes can generally be distinguished from other *Piranga* by their dark lores and grayish cheeks, nape, flanks, and back, all of which contrast against the reddish or yellowish color of other parts. The red of males is orange red rather than the bright red of male Summer Tanagers. Summer Tanagers often show a slight crest. Female Summer Tanagers are greenish with only a hint of gray and a darker lore, whereas the breast and forehead of female Hepatic Tanagers are a light orange yellow, with more gray in other parts and a distinctive dark lore.

Geographic variation   About fifteen subspecies are generally recognized (in three distinctive groups—see above). Of these, *P. f. hepatica* and *P. f. dextra* occur in our area. They are similar in appearance to other races in the *P. f. hepatica* subspecies group. *P. f. hepatica* breeds in Arizona and southwestern New Mexico whereas *P. f. dextra* breeds east of the Continental Divide. They are similar, but male *P. f. dextra* are more richly colored, and the gray on the sides of the face and flanks is reduced on females.

Distribution   *Breeds* from se California (where quite uncommon and local; San Bernardino and Kingston mountains, Clark Mountain, and probably the New York Mountains), nw and central Arizona, se and s-central Colorado (Prior), n New Mexico, w Texas, Nuevo León, and Tamaulipas south through the highlands of Central America to n-central Nicaragua and in Belize, extreme e Honduras, and ne Nicaragua.

Winters in central and s California (casual), s Arizona (casual), n Mexico, south in both highlands and lowlands through its breeding range. Casual elsewhere in California, Baja California, s Nevada, and sw Wyoming, and east to se Texas and sw Louisiana. Accidental in Illinois (Beverly).

In South America, *Piranga flava lutea* are **resident** in the mountains of northern South America (n Colombia, n Venezuela and also Trinidad), w Colombia, w Ecuador, s Venezuela, n Brazil, central Guyana, and central Surinam south to Peru, and on the east slope from n Peru south to Bolivia; *Piranga f. flava* are **resident** in e Brazil and s Guyana south through central and e Brazil to e Bolivia, n Argentina, w Uruguay, and se Brazil.

Conservation status   Hepatic Tanagers have been affected by habitat degradation because of human recreation and fires; they are threatened in El Savador.

Molt   A complete Prebasic molt occurs June through October; there may be some spring feather replacement, but the Alternate plumage is achieved principally through wear.

Description   Adult males—Reddish orange on crown, nape, throat and breast, and undertail coverts; lores dark, and ear coverts and flanks grayish; mantle grayish with orange red; *wings* and *tail* reddish gray. Adult females—Throat, and *tail* bright orangish yellow; crown, nape, mantle, and flanks grayish; *wing* feathers, including coverts, grayish, thinly edged in pale green (in unworn individuals). Juveniles are grayish and yellow, without any red feathers; outer coverts are narrow and tapered and brownish or buff yellow; there is brownish streaking over much of the body, and the *back* may be slightly barred; *underparts* are yellowish amber and the undertail coverts brownish yellow. *Bill* dark, with paler lower mandible, especially toward the base. *Legs* and *feet* blackish; *iris* black.

Hybrids   Mixed pairs of Hepatic and Flame-colored tanagers have been reported in southeastern Arizona, but there are no reports of hybrid offspring.

References   Eddleman (2002), Pyle (1997).

2.1 Male Hepatic Tanager *Piranga flava*, Santa Catalina Mountains, Arizona, USA, May 2001. A large tanager with a rather deep based, stout bill. Overall reddish, brightest on crown and throat, with dusky gray cast to mantle and wings. The auriculars are distinctively dusky gray, contrasting with dark lores. Bill is dark gray, darker on culmen (Brian E. Small).

2.2 Male Hepatic Tanager *Piranga flava*, Los Angeles, California, USA, December 2001. Rather similar to adult male Summer Tanager but note slightly duller plumage, gray bill, and dusky gray lores and auriculars. The head is rounded, lacking the slight crested appearance often evident on the Summer Tanager (Larry Sansone).

2.3 Female Hepatic Tanager *Piranga flava*, Patagonia, Arizona, USA, May 1998. Overall dull grayish olive, with yellow restricted to crown and breast. Similar to female Summer Tanager but duller overall, with a shorter dark gray bill. Note the dusky lores and grayish auriculars, creating a more contrasting head pattern. This bird was photographed in captivity (Rick and Nora Bowers).

3 Summer Tanager

(Piranga rubra)

Measurements
Length: 16.5–20 cm; 6.5–7.9 in.
Wing: 93–107 mm; 3.7–4.2 in. (males
slightly larger than females).
Mass: 28.2 g (Louisiana).

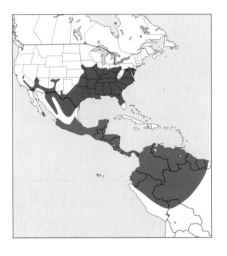

The Summer Tanager is a locally common Neotropical migrant that breeds in
southeastern North America and in the
American Southwest. Adult males are
rosy orange red, even on their wintering
grounds, with a yellowish or pale gray
bill, whereas females are dull greenish,
without noticeably dark wings (as female Scarlet Tanagers have). Males in
their first spring and summer are mottled red and green.

Habitat   In the East, Summer Tanagers breed in deciduous or pine-oak woodlands,
especially woodlands with sparse understory. Where they co-occur with Scarlet Tanagers, they generally are found in more open woodlands with less height and more
open canopy. In the Southwest, they are found in riparian woodlands, especially those
dominated by cottonwoods and willows. They overlap with Hepatic Tanagers in montane canyons.

Behavior   On their breeding grounds, Summer Tanagers are territorial, and generally found in pairs. When excited they raise their crown feathers, giving them a peak-
headed or slightly crested look. They may also be territorial in winter, where they generally are solitary but call frequently.

Voice   The song is a rambling series of two or three phrases and is robin-like. It is less
burry than that of the Scarlet Tanager. The call is a distinctive, staccato *pit-a-chuck*,
which is given year-round.

Similar species   The Hepatic Tanager is similar in color but males are a duller orange red rather than the bright rosy red of Summer Tanagers. Male Hepatic Tanagers
have a grayish mantle and gray on the flanks, whereas Summer Tanagers lack gray in
their plumage. Female Summer Tanagers have a greenish gray nape and sides of the
neck, whereas Hepatic Tanagers have grayish ear coverts, nape, mantle, and flanks. Female Hepatic Tanagers have dark lores, whereas those of Summer Tanagers are only
slightly grayish. The bill of Hepatic Tanagers is darker than that of Summer Tanagers,
and Hepatic Tanagers have slightly grayish ear coverts, and often some gray on their
mantle and flanks. Summer Tanagers often raise their crest feathers, giving their heads
a slightly peaked appearance.

Geographic variation Two subspecies are recognized, the eastern *P. r. rubra* and the western *P. r. cooperi* ("Cooper's" tanager). The latter is paler and a less deep red than the former, particularly on the underparts, and averages slightly larger. "Cooper's" tanagers, which have a noticeably larger bill than eastern Summer Tanagers, are found east to west Texas. Interestingly, all the Summer Tanagers that have been collected in San Diego County, in southern California, have been *P. r. rubra*, which do not generally occur west of the Great Plains.

Distribution *Breeds* from se California, s Nevada, Idaho (very rare), sw Utah, central Arizona, central New Mexico, central Texas, w-central Oklahoma, e Kansas, se Nebraska, South Dakota (very rare), s Iowa, central Illinois (rarely n Illinois), s Wisconsin, central Indiana, Ohio (rare in north), sw Pennsylvania, West Virginia, Virginia, e Maryland, and New Jersey south to ne Baja California, n Sinaloa, n Durango, se Coahuila, central Nuevo León, s Texas, the Gulf Coast, and s Florida. Rare in Oregon in summer (most records from Harney County).

Winters from s Baja California, s Sinaloa, and s Tamaulipas south through Central America and South America (including Trinidad) west of the Andes to s Ecuador and east of the Andes to n Bolivia and Amazonian Brazil. Rare in winter north to coastal Oregon, central and s California (most fall and winter specimens are *P. r. rubra*), s Arizona, Louisiana, s Florida, the Bahama Islands, and Cuba; vagrant on Hispaniola and the Lesser Antilles. Rare in fall and very rare in spring in s Quebec and Atlantic Canada; casual in winter north to Michigan, s Canada, and Newfoundland; there is a November record for North Dakota.

Accidental in Britain (Wales).

Conservation status Most populations of Summer Tanagers have remained stable over the past twenty-five years, although they have declined in numbers along the Colorado River in the Southwest.

Molt There is a partial First Prebasic molt of body feathers and some coverts from July or August into October, and a complete Definitive Prebasic molt in late summer that takes place on the breeding grounds. There is a partial First Prealternate molt, which includes some head and other body feathers, that occurs on the wintering grounds, November to March, and a partial Definitive Prealternate molt that excludes primaries; during the Definitive Prealternate molt, males acquire their Definitive Alternate red plumage.

Description **Adult males**—Bright rosy red (western birds average slightly duller), with outer webs of remiges somewhat darker. Males in their first spring variable but generally red, with many yellow contour feathers, especially posteriorly. **Adult females**—Like adult males but orangish or olive buff where males red, with some red body feathers (western females duller, without red in their plumage. **Immatures**—Males: crown and nape dull olive buff, streaked with gray; *rump* dull greenish buff and streaked with gray; rectrices cinnamon colored, edged with red; greater coverts olive grayish, tipped with yellow, forming a wing bar; *wings* olivaceous, with outer webs of primaries orangish brown; *underparts* whitish with patches of yellow and streaked with gray, especially on the breast. Females: like males but *tail* olivaceous and primaries lacking reddish edges. **Bill** gray brown to yellowish olive, often with paler tomia; *legs* and *feet* yellowish brown; *iris* dark brown.

Hybrids   A female paired with a male Scarlet Tanager was reported in Minnesota (2003), but no hybrid young were produced.

Reference   Robinson (1996).

3.1 Definitive Alternate male Summer Tanager *Piranga r. rubra*, Dry Tortugas, Florida, USA, April 1996. A large tanager with a rather long and stout horn-colored bill. Overall bright red, lacking contrasting head pattern of Hepatic Tanager. Note the uniformly red edges to all the wing feathers. Crown often with slight crested appearance (Kevin T. Karlson).

3.2 Female Summer Tanager *Piranga r. rubra*, Galveston, Texas, USA, May 2001. Overall more uniform greenish yellow than Hepatic Tanager. Head rather uniform, lacking contrasting dark lores and gray auriculars of Hepatic Tanager, though pale eye crescents often noticeable. Bill pale grayish horn (Brain E. Small).

3.3 First Alternate male Summer Tanager *Piranga r. rubra*, High Island, Texas, USA, May 1997. Highly variable, with a mixture of red and greenish yellow feathers on body; on this individual the wings and tail have entirely green-edged feathers (Brian E. Small).

3.4 First Alternate male Summer Tanager *Piranga r. rubra*, Dry Tortugas, Florida, USA, April 1999. Compared with the bird in figure 3.3, this individual has extensively red head and body plumage. The wings, though still mostly green, show some red edges to the inner median and greater coverts, outer secondaries, and middle tertials (Kevin T. Karlson).

3.5 Definitive Alternate male Summer Tanager *Piranga r. cooperi*, Riverside County, California, USA, May 1995. Western birds are virtually identical to birds from eastern populations but have, on average, slightly deeper-based, longer bills. More uniformly red than similar Hepatic Tanager, with less contrasting head pattern (Brian E. Small).

3.6 Female Summer Tanager *Piranga r. cooperi*, Patagonia, Arizona, USA, May 1998. Compared with similar-size Hepatic Tanager, note richer golden yellow and green plumage, with larger and paler bill and less contrasting head pattern (Rick and Nora Bowers).

4 Scarlet Tanager

(Piranga olivacea)

Measurements

Length: 16.5–18.0 cm; 6.5–7.1 in.

Wing: 90–101 mm; 3.5–4.0 in. (males slightly larger than females).

Mass: 17.5–35.2 g, av. 28.6 g (Pennsylvania, migrants).

The Scarlet Tanager is one of the more spectacular breeding species of the forest interior of northeastern North America, and one of relatively few North American breeding songbirds that principally winters in South America. These birds are strikingly sexually dimorphic in color: adult males are bright scarlet red, with black wings and tail, whereas females are a uniform dull olive green, with brownish wing and tail feathers. Males in winter are female-like in appearance but more brightly colored and have black in their wing coverts and remiges.

Habitat In migration and summer, Scarlet Tanagers are found in a wide variety of deciduous and mixed woods but prefer mature forests, especially where oaks are common, and in the Northeast may be found in pine-oak woods or oak-hemlock or oak-hickory woods. They also occur in beech woods and occasionally in pure stands of hemlock. They occasionally are found in extensive stands of planted shade trees in suburban gardens. In winter, they are often found in evergreen forests at middle elevations, and in the midcanopy of forests in foothills on the east slope of the Andes.

Behavior Scarlet Tanagers are generally solitary or, especially early in the breeding season, in pairs. In spring, males arrive before females, and there is some fighting and countersinging among males as territories are established. They are socially monogamous, and the pair bond is maintained through the breeding season. In winter, they tend to be solitary. They are strong flyers and sometimes hawk insects. They generally hop on the ground, but walk on the ground and on perches when searching for food.

Voice Their song is a series of four or five hoarse, burry phrases with a run-on robin-like pattern. Their call is a burry *chip-burr.*

Similar species The breeding (Definitive Alternate) males, which are bright red with black wings and tail, are unmistakable. The adult males in nonbreeding plumage resemble females but are brighter in color and have black wings and tail. Females and immatures may be confused with female or immature Summer or Western tanagers. The female Scarlet and Summer tanagers are best distinguished by their general coloration. Female Scarlet Tanagers are greenish in hue, with darker wings and tail, whereas female Summer Tanagers are more olive green, and adult females in the East often have red feathers admixed among the olive green ones. Female Western Tanagers have two yellowish or whitish wing bars (male Scarlet Tanagers can have buffy wing bars in winter but not bold, white ones), and some are decidedly grayish in color. Even female Scarlet Tanagers with narrow-winged birds can usually be distinguished from Western Tanagers, which have a grayer mantle. The call notes are distinctive: *chip-churr* or *chip-burr* for the Scarlet, and upslurred *pit-r-ick* or *pr-r-rick* for the Western, and *pit-a-chuck* for the Summer.

Geographic variation   None described.

Distribution   *Breeds* from central North Dakota, e Saskatchewan, s Manitoba, central Ontario, s Quebec (uncommon north of Lake Saint-John, s Gaspé), central Maine, s New Brunswick, and Nova Scotia south to central Nebraska, e Kansas, n-central and se Oklahoma, nw and n-central Arkansas, w-central Tennessee, se Oklahoma, nw and n-central Arkansas, w-central Arkansas, w-central Tennessee, n Alabama, n Georgia, nw South Carolina, w North Carolina, Virginia, and Maryland. Commonest in mountains from New Hampshire south to western North Carolina.

Winters from lowland Panama and Colombia south, east of the Andes through e Ecuador and Peru to n Bolivia. Reported in winter from Massachusetts, Colorado, and s California (late fall; one January record).

Migrates through e United States west to central Texas, rarely e Colorado and New Mexico, Central America, and the West Indies, and casually to the Rocky Mountains, Bermuda, and the Netherlands Antilles.

Casual in w North America from s British Columbia south to s Arizona (Patagonia), s California, Baja California, and Sonora, and in the Northeast to Prince Edward Island and Newfoundland. Accidental in Alaska (Point Barrow) and Clipperton Island, and in Iceland and the British Isles (September and October).

Conservation status   As a species that breeds in forest interiors, Scarlet Tanagers are sensitive to forest fragmentation, which leads to increased rates of both predation and brood parasitism, and in parts of their range they are found only in larger woodlands. However, breeding bird survey data show that they increased slightly in numbers between 1965 and 1979.

Molt   The Juvenal plumage is acquired by a Prejuvenal molt, June through August; there is a partial First Prebasic molt that includes body plumage and median coverts, and the inner greater coverts, July through September. There is a partial First Prealternate molt that includes body plumage, inner greater coverts, some tertials, and some or all of the rectrices; this molt takes place in January through March, beginning on the wintering ground. The Definitive Prebasic molt is complete and occurs on the breeding grounds, July through September; the Definitive Prealternate molt is incomplete and includes body feathers, inner greater coverts, and sometimes some central rectrices.

Description   Adult males—*Head, back, rump*, and *underparts* bright scarlet red; *wings* and *tail* black (a few have indistinct wing bars). **Adult females**—Similar to adult males but bright green or yellowish where male red, and *wings* and *tail* dull dark green; some older females can have quite reddish *heads*. **Males in fall and winter** like adult female but brighter, with black coverts and dusky *wings* and *tail*; some may have faint wing bars. **Females in fall and winter** like breeding females. **Juveniles** (of either sex) like females but duller. *Bill* pale gray or often orangish; *legs* and *feet* dusky; *iris* dusky.

Hybrids Scarlet Tanagers are reported to hybridize with Summer and Western tanagers. A male that paired with a female Summer Tanager in Minnesota (2003) failed to produce any hybrid young.

References Mowbray (1999), Pyle (1997), Robbins et al. (1986).

4.1 Definitive Alternate male Scarlet Tanager *Piranga olivacea*, Galveston, Texas, USA, May 2002. A smallish tanager with a moderately stout bill. Unmistakable. Shining, brilliant red head and body contrasting with deep velvet black scapulars, wings, and tail. Bill grayish. Uniform blackness of wings indicates this is an after-second-year male (Brian E. Small).

4.2 Definitive Alternate male Scarlet Tanager *Piranga olivacea*, High Island, Texas, USA, April 2001. There is some variation in the overall color of adult male Scarlet Tanagers. This individual is distinctly on the orange side of the scale relative to the bird depicted in figure 4.1 (Larry Sansone).

4.3 Female Scarlet Tanager *Piranga olivacea*, Galveston, Texas, USA, late April 2001. Overall olive green on head and upperparts, paler on underparts, and often rather yellow on face and upper breast. Wings and tail contrastingly dusky brown, with greenish feather edges. Similar to female Summer Tanager but smaller, with a relatively smaller bill and darker wings and tail (Brian E. Small).

4.4 First Alternate male Scarlet Tanager *Piranga olivacea*, Central Park, New York City, New York, USA, May 2001. Similar to Definitive Alternate male and likewise mostly red and black. Note marked contrast on wings between retained worn, green-edged primary coverts and flight feathers and fresh black coverts and tertials (Michael D. Stubblefield).

4.5 First Basic male Scarlet Tanager *Piranga olivacea*, Central Park, New York City, New York, USA, September 1998. Similar to female, but with scapulars and wing coverts deep velvety black, contrasting with the worn and brown primary coverts. Note also the bill is more pinkish orange than is typical for an adult bird (Michael D. Stubblefield).

5 Western Tanager

(Piranga ludoviciana)

Measurements
Length: 16.5–18.5 cm; 6.5–7.3 in.
Wing: 85–101 mm; 3.3–4.0 in. (males slightly larger than females).
Mass: 22.5–34.5 g, av. 28.1 g (California).

In its geographic distribution, the colorful Western Tanager is the western counterpart to the eastern Scarlet Tanager, although its closest relative may be the Flame-colored Tanager of Mexico. Like other *Piranga*, in summer it eats principally insects. However, at other times berries and fruit are important components of its diet.

Habitat   Western Tanagers are found in open coniferous woodlands, pine-oak woodlands, and aspen forests, primarily in mountains; they are often found in fairly open woodlands, especially Douglas fir, and may also occur in piñon-juniper woodlands. In winter, they occur singly or in small, loose flocks, in plantations and forest edges, and often around flowering eucalyptus in southern California.

Behavior   Although these are colorful birds with a loud, deliberate song, they are not generally conspicuous. Their movements are sluggish, and they tend to stay in foliage in trees. Males establish territories after arrival from the wintering grounds. Where their ranges overlap, they may exclude Hepatic and Flame-colored tanagers from their territories. They can be quite conspicuous as they hawk flying insects from the top of a tree. During migration, they are often solitary but may be found in small flocks containing, rarely, as many as thirty individuals. Outside the breeding season, they may associate with a variety of other species including chickadees, warblers, grosbeaks, orioles, and *Carpodacus* finches.

Voice   The song is similar to that of the Scarlet Tanager, a series of short discrete elements, resembling that of the American Robin in pattern, but hoarser: *pir-ri pir-ri pee-wi pir-ri pee-wi*. The calls are short and sometimes explosive: *pit-ick* or *pruree* or a rising *whee*.

Similar species   These are distinctive birds. Adult males are unmistakable. Females and First Basic males resemble Scarlet Tanagers but have either two white or one white and one yellow wing bar, and the backs of females are gray (as opposed to the greenish backs of female Scarlet Tanagers; some Scarlet Tanagers may have faint wing bars); Definitive Basic males in winter have much orange on their face. Pale adult females superficially resemble dull female Bullock's Orioles (but these have different bill shapes).

Geographic variation Most ornithologists treat the Western Tanager as monotypic.

Distribution *Breeds* from se Alaska (uncommon), s Yukon (rare), n British Columbia, s Mackenzie, n Alberta, and central Saskatchewan south to n Baja California, central and se Arizona, s New Mexico, and w Texas; also in North Dakota (casual), w South Dakota (Black Hills), and nw Nebraska. A singing male was seen near Thompson, Manitoba, in June 2003.

Winters from coastal s California, Baja California, and s Sonora and s Tamaulipas south through Mexico and Central America (mostly in the highlands; absent in the Yucatán Peninsula) south to Costa Rica and Panama (February 2004), and casually in the Gulf Coast region from se Texas and Arkansas east to s Florida, rarely north to s-central British Columbia, s Oregon, North Carolina, South Carolina, e-central Kansas, Mississippi, s Arizona, and s Texas.

Migrates east to w Nebraska, w Kansas, w Oklahoma, and central Texas.

Casual north to central Alaska, s Yukon, and the Queen Charlotte Islands, and across ne North America from Iowa and s Manitoba and Minnesota east through Wisconsin, Illinois, Michigan, s Ontario, and s Quebec to New Brunswick, Nova Scotia, and Newfoundland south to New York, Pennsylvania, Maryland, Virginia, and North and South Carolina. Accidental in n Alaska (Point Barrow), the Bahama Islands, Cuba, and Panama.

Conservation status Although the numbers of Western Tanagers vary locally from year to year, there are no clear long-term trends in their population. They are not considered to be threatened or endangered.

Molt There is a partial First Prebasic molt, involving body feathers and some coverts, that occurs July through September on the breeding grounds, and a partial First Prealternate molt that occurs mostly on the wintering grounds and involves rectrices but not remiges. The Definitive Prebasic molt is complete and takes place July through September (it may occur after a partial migration), and a partial Definitive Prealternate molt involves mostly anterior body feathers.

Description Adult males—Face, crown, and throat bright orange red, variable in extent; collar breast, *underparts*, and *rump* and uppertail coverts bright yellow; mantle and *wings* black, with yellow posterior lesser coverts and median coverts, and greater coverts broadly tipped with whitish or light yellow; tail black. Nonbreeding and first-year males duller, with little red on the head, and wings and *tail* black. Adult females—Greenish, often with gray *back* and *underparts* (underparts may be entirely yellow, and undertail coverts always yellow); *wings* and *tail* darker than body; whitish or pale yellowish median coverts and margins to greater coverts. First-year males resemble females but generally are brighter in color; they lack red on the *head*; replaced coverts are black, contrasting with the retained greenish Juvenal coverts, which are tipped with yellow; Definitive Basic males have reddish in the *head*, blackish *wings* and *tail*, and bright yellow *underparts*. Juveniles are like females. *Bill* olive or olive brown in juveniles, darker, often extensively orangish, in adult males; *legs* and *feet* medium gray; *iris* dark brown.

Hybrids Hybrids between Scarlet and Western tanagers have been reported (see the account of the Scarlet Tanager for details).

References Hudon (1999), Isler and Isler (1987), Pyle (1997).

5.1 Definitive Alternate male Western Tanager *Piranga ludoviciana*, Riverside County, California, USA, May 1999. Virtually unmistakable, with mostly black and yellow plumage. The head is variably orange red, blending into bright yellow collar and underparts. Note wide yellow bar on median coverts and white tips to greater coverts (Larry Sansone).

5.2 Female Western Tanager *Piranga ludoviciana*, Kern County, California, USA, May 2002. Structurally similar to Scarlet Tanager but note obvious whitish wing bars and grayish mantle. Note that the female Scarlet Tanager occasionally shows faint whitish wing bars. Females are variable in appearance, and this individual is rather drab and grayish overall. Bill is typically pale orange (Brian E. Small).

5.3 Female Western Tanager *Piranga ludoviciana*, Riverside County, California, USA, June 1999. A brighter individual than in figure 5.2, showing more extensive yellow on head and upper breast and some orange on forecrown and malar area. The median coverts show rather wide yellow tips. Note the contrast between the olive gray mantle and the olive yellow rump and head (Brian E. Small).

5.4 First Alternate male Western Tanager *Piranga ludoviciana*, Kern County, California, USA, May 2002. Similar to Definitive Alternate male but shows contrast between black wing coverts and tertials and worn brownish primary coverts and flight feathers. The blackish mantle is scalloped grayish olive, and the head shows less extensive orange red (Brian E. Small).

5.5 Basic Western Tanager *Piranga ludoviciana*, Santa Catalina Mountains, Arizona, USA, September 1992. Overall rather grayish, with yellow suffusion on head and rump. The wing pattern is distinctive, with pale yellow bar on median coverts and white tips to greater coverts and tertials. Fall birds in fresh plumage can be difficult to age and sex. The broadness of the pale tips to the wing coverts and the truncate tips to the primary coverts suggest this is an adult in fresh plumage. However, the tips to the tail feathers appear pointed. It is advisable to leave some birds as unsexed or of uncertain age (Rick and Nora Bowers).

6 Flame-colored Tanager

(Piranga bidentata)

Measurements
Length: 18.0–19.0 cm; 7.0–7.5 in.
Wing: 89–104 mm (sexes similar in size).
Mass: 33.3–39.4 g, av. 34.7 g (Mexico).

The Flame-colored Tanager is a bird of Mexican mountain canyons. It was first discovered in the United States in Cave Creek Canyon, Chiricahua Mountains, Arizona, in 1985; currently there are over a dozen records for southeastern Arizona as well as five records from Texas. Many individuals reported in the United States may be hybrids with Western Tanagers.

Habitat   These birds are found in oak-conifer woodlands in mountain canyons. They usually forage high in trees but will forage lower in fruiting trees. Rarely seen on the ground.

Behavior   Their behavior is doubtless much like that of the Western Tanager. They sometimes join mixed-species flocks.

Voice   The song is like the Western Tanager's but slower (about one note per second) and rougher, with longer pauses between elements. In Costa Rica, Flame-colored Tanagers often sing from the tops of isolated trees in pastures. The call is *prr-rt prr-rt*, much like that of the Western Tanager.

Similar species   See Western Tanager.

Geographic variation   *P. b. bidentata* is the only subspecies found north of Mexico. It can be distinguished by its relatively small bill (exposed culmen 15.1–17.7 mm); the head, throat, and breast of males are orange (compared to red in the other subspecies), and the breast of females is bright yellow (as opposed to dusky or orange). Also known as the Striped Tanager or Streak-backed Tanager.

Distribution   *Resident* from Sonora, s Chihuahua, central Nuevo León, and s Tamaulipas south through the interior of Mexico to n-central Nicaragua and the mountains of Costa Rica and w Panama.
 Breeds rarely in se Arizona (Chiricahua, Santa Rita, and Huachuca mountains; a pair nested successfully in Madera Canyon, Arizona, in 2004; *casual* elsewhere in s Arizona (e.g., Patagonia; fewer than ten records). Wanders very rarely east to Texas (five records, April and October; four records from Brewster and Jeff Davis counties) and to e Texas (South Padre Island).
 There are also several records of apparent hybrids with Western Tanagers in se Arizona.

Conservation status   This is a Mexican species that is extralimital in our area.

Molt   Probably like that of the Western Tanager; not described.

Description   Adult males—*Head*, throat, and breast bright orange; ear coverts dull orange, outlined in dusky; mantle blackish, streaked with orange. Scapulars orangish; greater coverts and tertials tipped with white. *Wings* dark with two distinct wing bars and large white spots on the tertials. *Tail* dark. Belly and undertail coverts yellow orange; flanks grayish. **Adult females**—Pattern similar to males but buffy yellow and yellow, with orange crown and streaked crown, mantle, and *rump*. *Bill* and *legs* and *feet* dark. *Iris* dark.

Hybrids   The Flame-colored hybridizes rather frequently with the Western Tanager at the northern edge of its range in Arizona. Hybrids with Western Tanagers are difficult to identify, as they resemble Flame-colored Tanagers. Male hybrids, however, tend to have some reddish on the face, yellowish underparts and rump, and a more or less solid black mantle. Also there is one record of a pairing with a Hepatic Tanager in southeastern Arizona.

References   Dunn et al. (2002), Lockwood and Freeman (2004).

6.1 Male Flame-colored Tanager *Piranga b. bidentata*, Madera Canyon, Arizona, USA, June 2004. Slightly larger and longer tailed than the similar Western Tanager, with more extensive orange on head and breast and grayish flanks. The longish, stout bill is wholly blackish, and the pale grayish auriculars are distinctively outlined blackish brown. Note also the boldly streaked mantle and white wing bars. This form is widespread in western Mexico and is a rare vagrant to Arizona (Brian E. Small).

6.2 Female Flame-colored Tanager *Piranga b. bidentata*, Madera Canyon, Arizona, USA, June 2004. Similar to male but head and underparts yellow. Head pattern as in male, with grayish lores and dusky edging to auriculars. Wings show bold white tips to median and greater coverts and tertials. Best distinguished from slightly smaller female Western Tanager by larger, blackish bill, head pattern, and boldly streaked mantle (Brian E. Small).

7 **Western Spindalis**

(Spindalis zena)

Measurements
Length: 15 cm; 6.0 in.
Wing: 69.5–84.0 mm; 2.7–3.3 in.
Mass: 17.0–25.5 g, av. 21.1 g.

These West Indian birds wander occasionally into southern Florida, where they are sometimes found in urban areas. Males are strikingly patterned, with black and white stripes on the head, an orange nape, and bold white greater coverts, but females are a rather drab grayish olive.

Habitat   In its native range in the West Indies, the Western Spindalis is found in open woodlands, shrubs on hillsides, and on mountains. In Florida, it is found in hardwood hammocks along the coast and in ornamental plantings in residential areas.

Behavior   These birds are arboreal and feed mostly on small fruits and buds, commonly low in bushes, but otherwise they tend to be found high in trees. In their flight display, they fly from the top of a tree and circle around, slowly beating their wings. They usually sing from a high perch.

Voice   The song is described as a prolonged, soft, high-pitched warble, *tsit-tsit-tsit*, or a high-pitched *see-tee*; its call a *seep*.

Similar species   This species resembles other West Indian *Spindalis* ("stripe-headed") tanagers, but this is the only species in that genus that occurs in our area.

Geographic variation   Formerly considered part of a polytypic species, *S. zena*, this species has been split from the Jamaican Spindalis (*S. nigricephala*), the Hispaniolan Spindalis (*S. dominicensis*), and the Puerto Rican Spindalis (*S. portoricensis*). Formerly known as the Stripe-headed Tanager.

Distribution   *Resident* in the Bahamas, Providenciales in the Turks and Caicos Islands, Cuba (including the Isle of Pines), Grand Cayman Island, and Cozumel Island (off Quintana Roo), Mexico. Irregular, rare to uncommon visitor to southern Florida (Monroe, Broward, and Palm Beach counties north to the Palm Beach area); all records September to June (July and August probably is the time of most breeding activity).

Conservation status   The Western Spindalis is common within its West Indian range.

Molt   No information available. Breeding occurs March through June (varies geographically), and molting probably occurs after breeding is concluded.

Description   Adult males—*Head* black, with white supercilium and moustacial stripe, black submoustacial stripe, and yellow throat; *back* black, with chestnut nape; *rump* yellowish, becoming chestnut posteriorly; *tail* black, with white edges to the outer two or more rectrices; *wing* black, with white edges to tertials, secondaries, and primaries, and at the base of the primaries; lesser and median coverts black, greater coverts black, boldly edged with white; ***underparts***, breast yellowish suffused with chestnut, becoming yellow posteriorly, and whitish on the belly and flanks; undertail coverts white; ***bill*** black, with grayish lower mandible with a dusky tip; ***legs*** and ***feet*** grayish dusky. **Adult females**—Plain olive above, pale olive gray below, with pale dusky supercilium and moustacial stripes, and dusky edged to greater coverts, tertials, and at the base of primaries; ***bill*** grayish; ***legs*** and ***feet*** gray; ***iris*** dark brown. **Juveniles**—like adult females but streaked on breast, belly, and flanks.

Hybrids   None reported.

References   Garrido et al. (1997), Raffaele et al. (1998), Ridgway (1902), Stevenson and Anderson (1994).

7.1 Male Western Spindalis *Spindalis zena*, Bahamas. A small tanager-like bird, with boldly patterned and colorful plumage. The bold black and white head pattern and wing markings are particularly conspicuous. Note also the silvery white underparts, contrasting with the rust and orange throat and breast (Kevin T. Karlson).

7.2 Female Western Spindalis *Spindalis zena*, Bahamas. Cryptically drab. Grayish olive upperparts relieved only by pale edges to wing coverts and tertials. There is a small whitish patch at the base of the primaries, but this feature is not visible in this photo. Underparts are pale gray suffused with olive on breast and flanks. Short, stout bill is grayish with pale base to lower mandible (Kevin T. Karlson).

8 Blue-gray Tanager

(Thraupis episcopus)

Measurements
Length: 143–147 cm; 5.6–5.8 in.
Wing: 80–90 cm; 3.1–3.5 in.
Mass: 27.0–45.0 g, av. 35 g.

Blue-gray Tanagers are among the most widespread and conspicuous of the New World tanagers. They were either intentionally or accidentally introduced into southern Florida but apparently have been extirpated there since the mid-1970s. Recent records are probably of escaped cage birds, and, at present, there does not appear to be a breeding population in the United States.

Habitat   Blue-gray Tanagers are common birds of woodland edges (including the margins of rivers), second growth, clearings, gardens, coffee plantations, and towns, from 0 to 2600 m, but only to 1500 m in Central America; they are most common in lowlands.

Behavior   Blue-gray Tanagers are generally seen in pairs or small groups, which might join passing mixed flocks of other species as these other species pass through their home range, but they do not stay with these flocks once they leave their area. At night, they often gather in large numbers to roost. Blue-gray Tanagers usually forage in the upper levels of trees but will pick up fallen fruit, and in Central America they are attracted to fresh fruit at feeders. They also glean insects and make quick aerial forays to capture flying insects.

Voice   The song is a slurred, squeaky, twittering *tsu tsu tseewee tseewee*. The most common call is a *chup* or *seee*. Sometimes two birds sing at the same time; female song is shorter and weaker than male song.

Similar species   Blue-gray Tanagers resemble Mountain Bluebirds in color; the race of Blue-gray Tanagers that was introduced into Florida, however, has whitish coverts.

Geographic variation   Several subspecies have been described. The birds introduced into southern Florida may have come from Brazil. Several races, including *T. e. coelestis*, occur in Brazil. *T. e. coelestis* have white on the wing coverts, as perhaps do some other Brazilian races; the one specimen from Florida that we have seen has white coverts.

Distribution   *Resident* from se San Luis Potosí, central Veracruz, and Oaxaca south (in lowlands) through Central America and in South America to nw Peru, n Bolivia, and Amazonian Brazil. Escaped or introduced to southern Florida in Hollywood, Broward County, in 1960, and nested at least there and in North Miami, and a specimen was collected in 1964 from Dade County. Blue-gray Tanagers have not been reported breeding in southern Florida since 1975, and more recent records are probably new escapees. A specimen of an adult female, collected 26 May 1964 at Coral Gables, Dade County, Florida, is in the collection of the University of Miami.

Conservation status Blue-gray Tanagers are not native to the United States and Canada. In its range, this common tanager is often kept as a caged bird.

Molt Blue-gray Tanagers have a long breeding season; molting probably occurs when the birds are not breeding, in late summer and fall.

Description **Adults** (sexes similar)—Pale dusty blue *head* and body with deeper blue *wings* (especially lesser coverts) and *tail*; wing tips blackish. In eastern Ecuador and Brazil, lesser and median coverts white; greater covers edged and tipped with white. **Juveniles**—Like adults, but with coverts gray. *Bill* dark, paler at base; *legs* and *feet* black; *iris* black.

Hybrids Hybrids with the closely related Palm Tanager have been reported.

References Isler and Isler (1987), Robertson and Woolfenden (1992), Skutch (1954), Stevenson and Anderson (1994), Wetmore et al. (1984).

8.1 Blue-gray Tanager *Thraupis episcopus cana*, Costa Rica, June 1985. A medium-size tanager with a moderately stout bill. Overall uniform pale bluish gray, with brighter blue edges to wing coverts and flight feathers. Lesser coverts vary in color. This form ranges from se Mexico to n Venezuela and has blue-edged lesser coverts. Reportedly at least some of the birds once established in Florida showed whitish lesser coverts, which is typical of birds from w and central Amazonia (Herbert Clarke).

9 Red-legged Honeycreeper

(Cyanerpes cyaneus)

Measurements
Length: 11–13 cm; 4.3–5 in.
Wing: 61–65 (av. 63) mm; 2.4–2.6 in.
Mass: 11.0–18.3 g, av.14 g.

Red-legged Honeycreepers are small Neotropical songbirds, with a slim and slightly decurved bill. Breeding males are patterned with black and blue, with bright red legs and yellow underwing coverts, which are noticeable in flight; females are dull greenish, with dull red legs. Within their range, they are locally common and easily seen.

Habitat   Red-legged Honeycreepers are found in tropical evergreen forests from sea level to 2000 m, mostly below 1200 m. They can be common in residential areas.

Behavior   Honeycreepers are often found in flocks, commonly of mixed-species composition, searching among flowers or foliage for food. When not foraging they sometimes perch on an exposed branch where they can easily be seen. They probe flowers for insects and nectar, and eat small berries and soft fruits. In Central America they frequently eat fruit at feeding tables.

Voice   The song is a hissing *zee* or *tsit*, or *dzi-dzi-deee*, *zzee*, or a *dee dee* that reminds one of a Black-capped Chickadee; they also utter a clear metallic note.

Similar species   The males, with their bright purplish blue coloration and bright red legs and feet, are unmistakable (to our knowledge, only males in breeding plumage have been reported from Florida). The Shining Honeycreeper is similar in color but has bright yellow legs. Female Red-legged Honeycreepers are dull greenish in coloration, with faint olive streaks on their breasts; female Shining Honeycreepers have distinct bluish streaks on their breasts and bluish caps and malar stripes.

Geographic variation   Several subspecies have been described. *Cyanerpes cyaneus carneipes* of eastern and southern Mexico is the subspecies that breeds in Cuba (where they may be introduced).

Distribution   *Resident* from se San Luis Potosí and central Veracruz, Guerrero (local), s Oaxaca, and Chiapas south (in lowlands) through Central America to nw Ecuador and locally to s Bolivia and central and se Brazil. Local and rather rare in Cuba; casual on Cozumel Island. Reported from Jamaica, and there are several recent reports from Florida (e.g., Biscayne National Park, 25–27 March 2003, Dry Tortugas National Park, 29 April–3 May 2003, Grassy Key, Florida, 2004), which may have been escaped cage birds.

Conservation status   Red-legged Honeycreepers are commonly kept as caged birds, but common in the wild in parts of their range.

Molt   This species molts after the breeding season (March to May). The males molt into a dull female-like plumage in June (they may be the only tropical passerine to have such an "eclipse" plumage); by October (in Costa Rica) they have acquired their blue plumage.

Description **Adult males**—Small, with a long, slightly decurved bill; crown bright turquoise blue, eye line and lores black; *back*, *wings*, and *tail* black; the rest of the body is bluish violet; wing lining bright yellow; *bill* black; *legs* and *feet* bright red; *iris* black. **Females**—Dull green, with a faint pale eye-line stripe and darker green *wings* and *tail*; the breast is faintly streaked with olive green; *legs* and *feet* are dull red. Post-breeding males are like females in coloration except that their wings and tail are black. **Juveniles** resemble adult females, with brown *legs* and *feet*.

Hybrids None reported.

References Isler and Isler (1987), North American Birds (2003), Raffaele et al. (1998), Skutch (1954), Wetmore et al. (1984).

9.1 Male Red-legged Honeycreeper *Cyanerpes cyaneus carneipes*, Chiapas, Mexico, June 1985. A small, rather slender tanager with a moderately long, slightly decurved bill. Mostly shining purplish blue with bright turquoise crown. Upperparts velvety black, with contrasting blue scapulars (just visible here). Black mask through eye. Legs bright pinkish red. In flight, underwing coverts and underside of flight feathers bright yellow. This form occurs in e and s Mexico (Herbert Clarke).

10 Crimson-collared Grosbeak

(Rhodothraupis celaeno)

Measurements
Length: 20–22 cm; 7.9–8.7 in.
Wing: 100–108 mm; 4.0–4.5 in.
Mass: No data available.

The Crimson-collared Grosbeak is endemic to northeastern Mexico and is found casually north in fall and winter to southern Texas. Most Texas records are of young or females, although males have been noted occasionally. These are rather long-tailed birds with a stout beak; young are dusky greenish with a blackish face; adult females are rather brighter with a contrasting black hood (although a green nape); adult males have a dark rose red on their breast and nape.

Habitat In Texas this tanager has been found only in deciduous thickets and gardens of the lower Rio Grande Valley, with the exceptions of birds seen near Laredo, Webb County, and Aransas Refuge, Aransas County.

Behavior Crimson-collared Grosbeaks skulk on or near the ground and often raise the feathers on the back side of the crown. On occasion, however, they may perch high in trees. Mostly single birds have been reported in Texas, but one group of three was recently discovered in Hidalgo County, where they were feeding on potato trees (*Solanum*). They may perch high in tall trees.

Voice The song is a varied warble, like that of the Black-headed Grosbeak but more variable, and ending with an upslurred *weeee*. The call is a strong, piercing *pweees*.

Similar species Unlike any other species in this area.

Geographic variation No geographic variation has been described.

Distribution *Resident* from e-central Nuevo León and s Tamaulipas south through e San Luis Potosí and n Veracruz to n Puebla. *Casual* in s Texas (Laredo, McAllen, Sabal Palm Audubon Sanctuary, Aransas National Wildlife Refuge). Until recently there were only nine records from Texas, all but one in fall and winter. However, in the winter of 2004–2005 there were at least 17 records from the Rio Grande Valley. One record (Hidalgo County) from 28 June to 1 July 1974.

Conservation status Extralimital in our area.

Molt Not described.

Description Adult males—*Head* and upper breast black; nape, collar, lower breast, and flanks a dull dark red; *wings* and *tail* black; undertail coverts dark, mottled with white. In flight, underwing coverts dull dark red. **Adult females**—Have a clearly delimited black hood like adult males, but with yellow olive *underparts* and olive *upperparts*. First-year females have a dusky face, with the black not clearly delimited by green. *Bill*, *legs* and *feet* dark; *iris* black.

Hybrids   None reported.

References   Dunn et al. (2002), Lockwood and Freeman (2004), Sibley (2000).

10.1 Female Crimson-collared Grosbeak *Rhodothraupis celaeno*, Gomez Farias, Mexico, October 2000. A chunky grosbeak, with longish tail and thick-based, stout bill. Mostly dull olive with olive yellow collar and underparts. Black head and upper breast forms a sharply demarcated hood. Thick, steel gray bill shows a markedly curved culmen. Nothing similar within its range (Rick and Nora Bowers).

11 Northern Cardinal

(Cardinalis cardinalis)

Measurements

Length: 16.5–21.0 cm; 6.5–8.3 in. (geographically variable; males somewhat
larger than females).
Wing: 81–99 mm; 3.2–3.9 in.
Mass: Male av. 45.4 g (33.7–63.2 g,
$n = 591$); female av. 51.7 g (33.6–
64.9 g, $n = 517$) (Pennsylvania).

The Northern Cardinal is one of the
most familiar songbirds throughout its
large North American range and is commonly seen in urban gardens and at
feeders. Sexually dimorphic in color, the
bright red males often sing their familiar
song from a conspicuous perch.

Habitat   Although throughout their range Northern Cardinals are found in open
thickets and woodland edges, at the northern part of their range they generally are associated with people who provide them with food in winter. In the Southwest they are
found in floodplain thickets and in thorn scrub.

Behavior   Cardinals are commonly found in pairs or small family groups. In high-
density areas, they may occur in small, loose flocks in winter. Despite their bright colors, they can stay well hidden in thickets. Individuals of both sexes sing, females generally from the nest. Their flight is undulating and often involves only short flights
between branches. Males play an active role in tending and feeding the young.

Voice   The song is a loud, musical series of warbles, variable but always distinctive,
such as *sweet sweet sweet sweet wit wit wit wit wit*; the *sweet sweet* elements tend to be
upslurred, and the *wit wit wit* notes accelerating. Another variant on this song consists
of several down-slurred whistles followed by accelerating *wit* notes: *wheet-a-low wheet-
a-low wheet-a-low wit wit wit wit wit wit wit wit*. Their contact call is a sharp *chip*.

Similar species   The Pyrrhuloxia of the Southwest has a similar size and shape, but
Pyrrhuloxia males are grayish with rosy red underparts, and the bill has a different
shape.

Geographic variation   Eighteen subspecies are commonly recognized. Of these,
five occur north of Mexico. The nominate *C. c. cardinalis* is resident in most of the eastern United States and southern Canada, and east of the western Great Plains. *C. c. flori-
danus*, which is found in southeastern Georgia and peninsular Florida, is smaller and
darker than *C. c. cardinalis*. *C. c. magnirostris*, of southern Louisiana and southeastern
Texas, is said to be larger with a larger bill than other eastern cardinals. *C. c. canicaudus*

of central and western Texas, south into Mexico, is similar. *C. c. superbus,* of southeastern California east to southwestern New Mexico and south into Mexico, is the largest of the races with a relatively stout bill, with the male's crest little if any duller in color than the breast; its crest is larger and fuller than that of eastern birds. The black of the lores of males does not meet across the forehead.

Distribution   *Resident* from central Baja California, se California (along the lower Colorado River, where rare; escapees occasionally are seen in other areas), central and se Arizona, s New Mexico, w and n Texas, se Colorado, w Kansas, w-central Nebraska, central and e North Dakota, se Manitoba (Winnipeg), central Minnesota, n Wisconsin, s Ontario, central Ontario (North Bay), s-central Quebec (Ottawa Valley; Montréal area), n New York, New Brunswick (rare, but increasing), and s Nova Scotia south to s Baja California Sur, Sonora, Tres Marias Islands (off Nayarit), Guanajuato and Hildago east to Veracruz, the Yucatán Peninsula, central Belize, and n Guatemala, and to the Gulf Coast and s Florida (including the Keys). Also along the Pacific Coast of Mexico, from Colima south to Oaxaca. In winter reported north to central Alberta (Edmonton) and Saskatchewan (Theodoe, Saskatoon). Introduced into El Monte, Los Angeles County, California, in about 1920, but only a few are left.

Conservation status   Throughout most of its range the Northern Cardinal is a common species. In the past hundred years its range in the Northeast has expanded northward, probably largely in response to winter feeding but perhaps in part because of climatic amelioration. In the early 1900s Northern Cardinals were common in Pennsylvania and New Jersey but had been reported from only two New York counties. Between 1940 and 1960 they moved into New England, and first nested in Massachusetts in 1958. They were first reported in Michigan in 1884 and were common there by 1909. Cardinals were first collected in Ontario in 1849 and were found nesting there by 1901. Today, they are found north to Thunder Bay, Kirkland Lake, and Ottawa, Ontario, and into southern Quebec. Nesting first confirmed in New Brunswick in 1980. Since 1970 they have been in Newfoundland, where they are rare.

Molt   While still in the nest or shortly after fledging, most or all of the body feathers (except for some coverts) are replaced by a Supplemental molt. The First Basic plumage is acquired by a partial Prebasic molt, from May through the summer. The Definitive Basic plumage is acquired by a complete Definitive Basic molt, from August through November.

Description   Adult males—Bright red throughout except for a black face, throat, and black around the eye; *wings* and *tail* somewhat darker red; there is a grayish wash on the mantle and flanks. **Adult females**—Like males in color but grayish tan rather than red, with belly and undertail coverts grayish; crest, *wings*, and *tail* dull reddish. **Juveniles** like females, duller, without red in crest. *Bill* bright red (blackish in juveniles); *legs* and *feet* medium brown; *iris* dark brown or black.

Hybrids   In the Southwest, Northern Cardinals are often found with Pyrrhuloxias, and the two species often have overlapping territories. There is a record from Arizona of a female hybrid between these two species.

Reference   Halkin and Linville (1999).

11.1 Male Northern Cardinal *Cardinalis c. cardinalis*, Texas, USA, April 1995. Large and long tailed with long, expressive crest. Overall bright red, with contrasting black lores and chin. The large, thick-based bill is strikingly orange red. The nape, mantle, and wing coverts appear dusted with reddish gray (Greg W. Lasley).

11.2 Female Northern Cardinal *Cardinalis c. cardinalis*, Rio Grande, New Jersey, USA, January 2003. Notably duller than adult male, with head and body brownish; warmer buffy cinnamon on face, breast, and flanks. Tip of crest, wings, and tail reddish. Lores and feathers around the orange bill grayish (Kevin T. Karlson).

11.3 Female Northern Cardinal *Cardinalis c. cardinalis*, Orono, Ontario, Canada, December 1990. Some females, perhaps older individuals, can show an extensive reddish wash on breast and face, usually with some red above the eye. Otherwise note the overall warm colors and reddish wings, tail, and tip of (depressed) crest (James Richards).

11.4 Male Northern Cardinal *Cardinalis c. superbus*, Tucson, Arizona, USA, February 2000. Similar to eastern populations, but with larger and fuller crest and slightly more curved culmen. Black on face reduced, especially above bill (Rick and Nora Bowers).

11.5 Female Northern Cardinal *Cardinalis c. superbus*, Tucson, Arizona, USA, October 1991. Virtually identical to female from eastern populations. Note the overall cinnamon brown appearance, with large, deep-based, orange red bill and reddish wings and tail (Rick and Nora Bowers).

11.6 Juvenile Northern Cardinal *Cardinalis c. superbus*, Tucson, Arizona, USA, September 1999. Similar to adult female, but with more extensive pale cinnamon on face and underparts and lacking red on tips of crest feathers. Face lacks any gray or black around bill, giving a "beady-eyed" appearance. Bill is blackish rather than orange red (Rick and Nora Bowers).

1 2 Pyrrhuloxia

(Cardinalis sinuatus)

Measurements
Length: 17.5–21.4 cm; 6.9–8.4 in.
(males slightly larger than females).
Wing: 88–99 mm; 3.5–3.9 in.
Mass: 29.7–44.0 g; male av. 36.7 g, fe-
male av. 34.3 g (Arizona).

The Pyrrhuloxia is a resident of the
desert scrub in the southwestern United
States and northern Mexico. It is closely
related to the Northern Cardinal, which
also breeds in that area, although often
in wetter areas than the Pyrrhuloxia.
Pyrrhuloxias have expanded their range
in Texas during the past hundred years,
probably following the northward inva-
sion of honey mesquite. The distinctive
thick, curved, and pale bill helps to distinguish Pyrrhuloxias from the cardinals.

Habitat   In Arizona and Sonora, Pyrrhuloxias are found in upland Sonoran Desert
habitats, 1000–1500 m, especially mesquite-dominated desert scrub, and also in riparian woodlands. They also breed in residential and agricultural areas, especially where
mesquite grows. In southern Texas they are found in mesquite grasslands. Especially
in winter, they are found at feeders.

Behavior   During the breeding season, Pyrrhuloxias are territorial, but their territories may overlap those of Northern Cardinals. In winter, they form feeding and roost-
ing flocks (often with cardinals); these flocks may consist of up to fifty individuals, and
they may wander some distance.

Voice   The song of the Pyrrhuloxia resembles that of the Northern Cardinal but is
sharper and perhaps higher. The call is a sharp metallic *cheek* or *chink* that is slightly
longer than that of the cardinal. In Arizona, cardinals and Pyrrhuloxias may countersing (that is, one sings and the other returns song).

Similar species   The Pyrrhuloxia most closely resembles the Northern Cardinal but
is not so red. Ventrally, male Pyrrhuloxias are rosy red (not bright scarlet red), and the
bill is yellowish (the cardinal's is red) and strongly curved (the cardinal's is cone-
shaped). Female Pyrrhuloxias have much less red in their wings and tail than female
cardinals, and it is restricted to the edges of the primaries and coverts and the lateral
rectrices. Note also the differences in bill shape and color (female Pyrrhuloxias have a
yellowish gray bill, whereas cardinal's bill is red). Juvenile Pyrrhuloxias are grayish,
whereas juvenile cardinals are a richer rosy brown color; the bill of young cardinals is
black, becoming red as they age.

Geographic variation Three subspecies have been described. *C. s. sinuatus* breeds in the Chihuahuan Desert of southeastern Arizona east into southern New Mexico and Texas. This race is larger than *C. s. fulvescens*, which is found in the Sonoran Desert of southern Arizona. A third subspecies is found in Baja California.

Distribution *Resident* from central Baja California, Sonora, s Arizona, and s New Mexico east to w and s-central Texas, south to s Baja California Sur, n Nayarit, n Jalisco, n Michoacán, Querétaro, se San Luis Potosí, and s Tamaulipas. *Casual* north to s California (San Miguel Island and north to Los Angeles and San Bernardino counties), central Arizona, central New Mexico, Colorado, sw Kansas, e-central Texas, and extreme w Oklahoma. In winter, they sometimes gather in wandering flocks and may wander (migrate?) quite a long distance. There is a winter record from s Ontario (Eagle, 2004–2005); this bird may have been an escapee or have been transported north by a truck.

Conservation status The Pyrrhuloxia is neither threatened nor endangered. Clearing brush in Texas has locally decreased suitable habitat, as has the growth of cities in Arizona.

Molt There is a partial or complete Supplemental molt that takes place early in life, from mid-April through September. The First Prebasic plumage is acquired by a partial to complete Prebasic molt. The Definitive Basic plumage is acquired by a complete Prebasic molt that occurs late July through September.

Description **Adult males**—Gray, with rosy red crest, face, midbelly, primaries, and lateral rectrices, and grayish brown on the mantle. **Adult females**—Like adult males but grayish yellow, with reduced red in the face, crest, *wings*, and *tail*, and none on the belly. **Juveniles** like females but much duller, with a gray brown bill. *Bill* yellow to orange in males, duller in females; *legs* and *feet* dull light brown; *iris* dark brown.

Hybrids A hybrid with a Northern Cardinal was found in Arizona.

References Lockwood and Freeman (2004), Sibley (2000), Tweit and Thompson (1999).

12.1 Spring male Pyrrhuloxia *Cardinalis sinuatus*, Roma, Texas, USA, May 2002. Large and longish tailed with pointed crest and thick-based, stubby bill. Mostly midgray, strikingly marked with bright red on crest, face, and central underparts. Primaries and outer tail feathers reddish. The rather short, yellow bill has a strongly curved culmen (Brian E. Small).

12.2 Basic male Pyrrhuloxia *Cardinalis sinuatus*, Tucson, Arizona, USA, February 1992. In this front view, note the rosy red face contrasting with the stubby, pale yellow bill. The underparts are mostly midgray, with rosy red suffusion along center of breast and belly (Rick and Nora Bowers).

12.3 Female Pyrrhuloxia *Cardinalis sinuatus*, Falcon Dam, Texas, USA, February 1998. Differs from male in being mostly dull grayish brown, paler on underparts. Reddish color is much reduced on crest, wings, and tail. Differs from female Northern Cardinal in "colder" gray appearance and stubby, more rounded pale yellow bill (Kevin T. Karlson).

12.4 Female Pyrrhuloxia *Cardinalis sinuatus*, Roma, Texas, USA, December 1994. On this winter bird note that the bill color is more grayish, with distinctly darker culmen. Otherwise, general plumage remains similar to that of summer birds (Brian E. Small).

1 3 **Yellow Grosbeak**

(Pheucticus chrysopeplus)

Measurements
Length: 21.3–24.1 cm; 8.4–9.5 in. (males slightly larger than females).
Wing: 106–124 mm; 4.2–4.9 in.
Mass: 54.0–77.6 g, av. 62.7 g (Peru = *P. chrysogaster*).

The Yellow Grosbeak is a Mexican and Central American species that only occasionally occurs north into Arizona and New Mexico. With the exception of one record from October, all records are from early June through late July.

Habitat   In southern Sonora the Yellow Grosbeak is a common species in tropical deciduous forests, especially where there are large trees along watercourses. In Arizona all records have been from montane canyons in the southeastern and south-central part of the state. One individual, seen in October in the desert lowlands in Tucson, was probably an escaped cage bird.

Behavior   Like other *Pheucticus* grosbeaks, males often sing their striking song from a conspicuous perch in a tree, and their song and bright coloration makes them conspicuous. They only rarely wander north into the United States, where only single individuals have been reported.

Voice   The song is similar to that of the Black-headed Grosbeak but slower and lower. The call is a sharp *pik*.

Similar species   Unlike any other species in our area, although Yellow Grosbeaks can be confused with Evening Grosbeaks.

Geographic variation   *P. chrysogaster* of South America is considered conspecific by some authors.

Distribution   *Breeds* from s Sonora (north to central Sonora in summer), sw Chihuahua, Sinaloa, and w Durango south in highlands to n Guerrero, Morelos, w Puebla, and central Oaxaca, and in s Chiapas and central Guatemala. In *winter* it withdraws from the northern part of its range. *Casual* in central and s Arizona and New Mexico (Santa Fe County, 18–21 October 2002). Several records from California are thought to be of escapees.

Conservation status   Extralimital in our area, but they are relatively common in their range in Mexico.

Molt   Not described, but probably like that of other *Pheucticus* grosbeaks.

Description   Adult males—*Head*, mantle, and **underparts** bright lemon yellow; undertail coverts white. *Wings* black with white-tipped greater and median coverts, and prominent white bases to the primaries; tertials with white spots. Uppertail coverts black with white spots; *tail* black with broad white tips to the outermost three rectrices. **Adult females**—Like adult males but duller yellow, mantle greenish, streaked with black, with some dusky streaking on the nape and crown; *wings* and *tail* brownish rather than black; reduced white in the bases of the primaries. *Bill*, *legs*, and *feet* black; *iris* black.

Hybrids   No hybridization reported.

References   Dunn et al. (2002), Russell and Monson (1998), Sibley (2000).

13.1 Male Yellow Grosbeak *Pheucticus chrysopeplus*, Arizona-Sonora Desert Museum, Tucson, Arizona, USA, November 1989. A large, stocky grosbeak with a large head and heavy, grayish bill. Golden yellow head and body, with contrasting black wings and tail. Bold white spots on wing coverts, tertials, and upper tail coverts create a striking pattern. Not likely to be confused with other grosbeaks (Rick and Nora Bowers).

13.2 Male Yellow Grosbeak *Pheucticus chrysopeplus*, El Triunfo, Chiapas, Mexico, March 2003. On this profile note the massive, steel gray bill, large, blocky head, and rather short tail. Wings mostly black, with bold white tips to coverts, tertials, and patch at base of primaries (Greg W. Lasley).

13.3 Female Yellow Grosbeak *Phecticus chrysopeplus*, Arizona-Sonora Desert Museum, Tucson, Arizona, USA, April 1998. Duller than male, with olive suffusion on crown, auriculars, and mantle. Crown and upperparts streaked with black. Wings duller than male's, but still with bold white wing bars and tertial spots. Best distinguished from other grosbeaks by mostly yellow face and underparts (Rick and Nora Bowers).

14 Rose-breasted Grosbeak

(Pheucticus ludovicianus)

Measurements
Length: 16.5–18.3 cm; 6.5–7.5 in. (sexes similar in size).
Wing: 90–110 mm; 3.5–4.3 in.
Mass: 35.4–65.0 g, av. 45.6 g (Pennsylvania).

The colorful Rose-breasted Grosbeak is one of the most conspicuous woodland birds of the Northeast. Sexually dimorphic in color, the adult males have a bright rose pink breast that contrasts with their otherwise black head, wings, and tail, and white underparts.

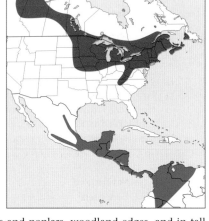

Habitat Rose-breasted Grosbeaks breed in a variety of open deciduous or mixed woodlands, especially cottonwoods and poplars, woodland edges, and in tall second growth. In migration they are found in a variety of woodland habitats.

Behavior Rose-breasted Grosbeaks are nocturnal migrants and are found singly or in small, loose flocks (of up to fifty individuals in Panama). In spring, males arrive before females, and older males generally before first-year males. Soon after arrival, males start to establish territories, and song is important in establishing and maintaining territories; passing migrant males remain silent when on an established male's territory. They are apparently monogamous, and individuals of both sexes attend to the nest and young. Females may sing when nest building or brooding. They hop when on the ground or on a branch.

Voice The song is a run-on series of melodious phrases, like that of the American Robin but faster and steady in cadence; the primary song is nearly identical to that of the Black-headed Grosbeak. The most common call note is a distinctive metallic *chink* or *eek*; this has a squeakier quality than the note of the Black-headed Grosbeak. They also have a whistled *phew* note, and fledged juveniles give a slurred *see-oo* note.

Similar species Adult males are distinctive, but females resemble female Black-headed Grosbeaks. Female Rose-breasted Grosbeaks, however, have bold streaks on their whitish or buffy breast, whereas female Black-headed Grosbeaks have thin streaks on a yellowish breast. The ventral streaking, however, is variable, and—especially in worn birds—can be difficult to assess. As well, females and first-fall males frequently have a band of buff across their breast, especially in fall in fresh plumage. The color of the underwing coverts differs between the two species, being "saffron yellow" to yellow buff in Rose-breasted and bright "lemon-yellow" in Black-headed grosbeaks. However, while this difference is useful if direct comparisons in the hand are possible, it is difficult to detect in the field. Perhaps the most useful field feature is the bill color: female Rose-breasted Grosbeaks have bills that are entirely pale pink or whitish, whereas female Black-headed Grosbeaks generally have gray bills, especially the upper mandible. Adult male Rose-breasted Grosbeaks have whitish bills, whereas Black-headed Grosbeaks have dark upper mandibles. First-winter Rose-breasted males are very much like adult female Black-headed Grosbeaks but have salmon pink to bright rose underwing coverts; immature male Black-headed Grosbeaks may have pink on their lower mandibles, but the upper mandible is darker.

Geographic variation   None described.

Distribution   *Breeds* from ne British Columbia, sw and s-central Mackenzie, n Alberta, central Saskatchewan, s Manitoba, central Ontario, s Quebec (north to Lake Saint-John, Sept-Îles, including Magdalen Islands), New Brunswick, Prince Edward Island, Nova Scotia, Newfoundland, and St. Pierre south to central and se Alberta, s Saskatchewan, n-central North Dakota, e South Dakota, central Nebraska, central Kansas, e Oklahoma, s Missouri, s Illinois, central Indiana, s Ohio, Massachusetts (absent from Nantucket Island), e Kentucky, e Tennessee, n Georgia (above 850 m), w North Carolina, w Virginia, West Virginia, Maryland, and Delaware, and casually west to e Wyoming, ne Colorado, New Mexico, Arizona, and central California (mostly coastal).

Winters from Nayarit and se San Luis Potosí south through Central America to n and e Colombia, Venezuela, Ecuador, and e-central Peru, rarely in s Texas, s Louisiana, s Mississippi, s Alabama, w Cuba, and Bermuda; occasionally seen in breeding range in winter (north to New Brunswick, Ontario, New York, and Michigan) and in Oregon (very rare, mostly early March through July), coastal Washington, Utah, California (rare, but regular in s California), and se Arizona (rare) south to Sonora (three records) and central Baja California, and north to Alaska (five records, fall).

Migrates east of the Rockies, ne Mexico, and irregularly through Bermuda, the Bahamas, the Greater Antilles, the Cayman Islands, and islands in the w Caribbean Sea, and casually through w North America from s British Columbia, Idaho (rare), and Montana south to Arizona and nw Mexico.

Casual or accidental in the Lesser Antilles, Greenland, the British Isles (twenty-one records, mostly from October), Sweden, France, Spain, Yugoslovia, and Malta; sight records from ne Alaska, se Alaska (Juneau, October), and the Revillagigedo Islands, Mexico.

Conservation status   The Rose-breasted Grosbeak is not listed as threatened or endangered in any part of its range, but it is a popular cage bird in Central America. These birds prefer younger forests, so their numbers may decline in areas as forest maturation occurs.

Molt   The Rose-breasted Grosbeak probably has a Presupplemental molt, June through September, followed by the First Prebasic molt in late summer or early fall. The Presupplemental molt involves many body feathers, which may be replaced again in the First Prebasic molt. Individuals in the First Prebasic plumage closely resemble Definitive Basic females. The First Prealternate molt is variable and takes place during winter and spring, before migration; it involves coverts, tertials, perhaps some secondaries and rectrices, and perhaps is less extensive in females than males. First Alternate males resemble Definitive Alternate males, except that some Juvenal primaries and coverts are retained, as sometimes are some of the brownish First Basic feathers. First Alternate females resemble First Basic females, but their remiges are more worn. The Definitive Basic plumage is acquired by a complete molt during the summer, which starts on the breeding grounds but may be completed in September or later, perhaps during the final stages of migration.

Description   Adult males—In summer (Alternate plumage), *head*, throat, upper part of breast, and mantle black; *wings* black, with broad white bases on both the inner and outer webs of the primaries; tips of the median coverts broadly white, forming a broad white wing bar; tips of inner and sometimes all greater coverts with white spots, forming a second wing bar; secondaries and tertials with small white spots, sometimes lost through wear; axillaries and underwing coverts bright pinkish red; *tail* black with white inner webs to outermost rectrices; *rump* and upper tail coverts white, with black flecks; undertail coverts white; breast with a broad, triangular patch of bright pink (rose); *underparts* otherwise white. Adult males in winter (Basic plumage) like summer males, but with buffy tips to many of the *head* and *back* feathers, and a buffy postocular stripe and buffy tips to the rump feathers; indistinct dark flecks on the flanks. Adult females—(Basic plumage) *head* and crown dull black, with feathers edged in olive brown; a distinct pale median crown stripe and, bordering the brown, lateral crown stripes to the nape; mantle dark brown, with paler edges to feathers; *wings* blackish brown with varying amounts of white in the outer webs of the bases of the primaries; greater coverts and tertials with narrow white or buff tips, forming two wing bars; underwing coverts yellowish to salmon pink, rarely as brightly pink as in males; *tail* dark brown with white tips to the inner webs of the outer rectrices; *rump* dark brown, mottled with buff; undertail coverts whitish. Females in Alternate plumage similar to females in Basic plumage. First-winter males resemble adult females but are brighter with broader wing bars and brighter pink axillaries and underwing coverts than most females, and perhaps richer color on the breast. *Bill* of adults pink white to slate gray, paler on the lower mandible; *legs* and *feet* grayish blue to slate brown; *iris* dark brown.

Hybrids   Hybridizes regularly but not commonly with the Black-headed Grosbeak in northwestern Kansas, central Nebraska, central South Dakota, and central North Dakota.

References   Morlan (1991), Rising (1983), Sibley (2000), Wyatt and Francis (2002).

14.1 Definitive Alternate male Rose-breasted Grosbeak *Pheucticus ludovicianus*, Galveston, Texas, USA, May 1998. A hefty, large-billed grosbeak with relatively short tail. Velvety black upperparts and hood contrast with white rump (not visible here) and underparts. Conspicuous rose red, inverted triangle on breast. White wing bars and patch at base of primaries. Note also blackish spotting on rear flanks and wholly pale bill (Brian E. Small).

14.2 Female Rose-breasted Grosbeak *Pheucticus ludovicianus*, Galveston, Texas, USA, May 2000. Mostly streaky brown upperparts contrast with whitish underparts. Note coarse, dusky streaking on breast and flanks and boldly striped head pattern. Wing coverts and tertials are tipped whitish. Best distinguished from similar female Black-headed Grosbeak by paler streaked underparts and uniform pale bill and by buff to dull yellow underwing coverts when visible; these are bright lemon yellow in Black-headed Grosbeaks (Brian E. Small).

14.3 First Alternate male Rose-breasted Grosbeak *Pheucticus ludovicianus*, Dry Tortugas, Florida, USA, April 1997. Similar to adult male, but with primary coverts and flight feathers worn and brown, thus contrasting with fresh black wing coverts and tertials. Some birds can show considerable pale mottling on head and upperparts (Kevin T. Karlson).

14.4 First Basic male Rose-breasted Grosbeak *Pheucticus ludovicianus*, New York City, New York, USA, August 2002. Similar to adult female, but with buffier breast and flanks with much finer streaking and variable suffusion of red on breast. Just visible are the distinctive red underwing coverts. First-winter male Black-headed Grosbeak similar, but with uniformly unstreaked, deeper orange underparts and yellow (if visible) underwing coverts (Michael D. Stubblefield).

14.5 Basic female Rose-breasted Grosbeak *Pheucticus ludovicianus*, New York City, New York, USA, September 2001. Like spring female, but with extensive buffy suffusion on underparts. Distinguished from female Black-headed Grosbeak by more coarsely streaked breast and flanks (Michael D. Stubblefield).

15 Black-headed Grosbeak

(Pheucticus melanocephalus)

Measurements
Length: 18.0–20.5 cm; 7.0–8.0 in. (sexes
similar in size).
Wing: 90–110 mm; 3.5–4.5 in.
Mass: 35.0–48.8 g; male av. 41.8 g, fe-
male av. 42.2 g (California).

The Black-headed Grosbeak replaces the
closely related eastern Rose-breasted
Grosbeak in western North America.
Both are quite variable in plumage, and
females of the two species can be difficult to distinguish.

Habitat   Black-headed grosbeaks are
found in a variety of open woodlands,
including riparian cottonwoods, pon-
derosa pine forest, pine-oak woodlands, oak scrub, and piñon-juniper. They often are
seen fairly high in trees. In migration, they occur in many types of woodlands.

Behavior   During the breeding season, Black-headed Grosbeaks are highly territorial
and apparently monogamous. Upon arrival in the spring, males establish territories by
singing and chasing away other males. When their arrival in spring coincides with
large hatches of crane flies, they can be conspicuous as they hawk the flies from the
top of a tree. During migration and winter, however, they are less aggressive and are
often found in loose flocks. They hop when on the ground.

Voice   The song is a musical series of loosely connected phrases, robin-like but less
harsh. It is nearly identical to that of the Rose-breasted Grosbeak, although it is sometimes said that it is lower pitched and more rapid. Females often sing. The call is a
harsk *kichk* or *chink* (the Rose-breasted's note is squeakier). They also give a whistled
phew note, and fledged juveniles a slurred *see-oo* note.

Similar species   Adult male Black-headed Grosbeaks are unmistakable, but first-
winter males and females can closely resemble Rose-breasted Grosbeaks. Breast color,
underwing color, and streaking generally differentiate these two species (see details in
the account of the Rose-breasted Grosbeak), but not all individuals can be distinguished by those features. Bill color can be a good field character: Rose-breasted Grosbeaks have pale pink or whitish bills, whereas Black-headed Grosbeaks have a more
dusky bill.

Geographic variation   Two subspecies are recognized. *P. m. maculatus* breeds along
the Pacific Coast from southwestern British Columbia south to Baja California. Its
wings average somewhat shorter than those of *P. m. melanocephalus*, which breeds

throughout the rest of the species' range, and *P. m. maculatus* has, on average, a shorter bill. The two subspecies are weakly differentiated.

Distribution   *Breeds* from coastal s British Columbia, s Alberta, s Saskatchewan, ne Montana, and central North Dakota south to n Baja California, s California, s Nevada, central and se Arizona, and, in the highlands, to Guerrero and Oaxaca (west of the Isthmus of Tehuantepec), and east to w South Dakota, w Kansas (rarely east to Cloud and Pottawatomie counties and Kansas City), e New Mexico, and w Texas.

Winters from Washington (three records), coastal California (rare), s Baja California, se Arizona (rare or casual), n Mexico, se Texas, and s Louisiana (rare) south to central Oaxaca, Veracruz, and rarely to Costa Rica; most winter from s Sonora southward. Spring migration starts in mid-March, and fall migration in mid-July.

Casual or rare in e North America from s Manitoba, Minnesota, Wisconsin, Michigan, w and s Ontario, sw Quebec, New York, Maine, New Brunswick, and Nova Scotia south to the Gulf Coast and Florida; also casual in se Alaska (fall) and Middleton Island, Alaska.

Conservation status   Black-headed Grosbeaks have benefited locally from some human activities such as irrigation, creation of orchards, and creation of openings in woodlands. In Mexico they are kept as caged birds, but these numbers are probably too small to have any overall effect on populations.

Molt   Detailed information on the timing of molts is not available, but the molts are doubtless much like those of the Rose-breasted Grosbeak. The First Prebasic molt is partial and does not include remiges, rectrices, or coverts; this molt starts in summer and is continued in migration and winter. The First Prealternate molt is partial and highly variable (especially in males, for some of which it is nearly complete). The Definitive Basic molt is complete and takes place on the wintering grounds. The Definitive Alternate molt is partial and includes only body feathers; it takes place before the return to the breeding grounds.

Description   Adult males—*Head* black from bill to nape; the black may be broken by a variable cinnamon yellow eye-line stripe extending from behind the eye; nape, collar, *underparts*, and *rump* cinnamon yellow; primaries black, with the basal parts (except for the ninth) white, forming a bright white patch in flight and when sitting; secondaries black, tipped with white; greater and median secondary coverts tipped in white; underwing coverts lemon yellow; rectrices black with broad white tips to outer ones (outermost are almost entirely white, with less white on inner ones). **Adult females**—Drab brown and buff, with a whitish to yellowish supercilium and malar stripe; crown brownish black with a pale, irregular median crown stripe; *wings, tail,* and *rump* brown, with dull buffy streaking on the mantle and pale tips to secondaries, forming two indistinct wing bars; *underparts* orangish buff with faint or weak streaking on the flanks; undertail coverts light brownish buff. **First-winter males** like adult females but much brighter ventrally, without streaking. *Bill* brown or slate colored; *legs* and *feet* slate colored; *iris* dark brown.

Hybrids   Black-headed Grosbeaks hybridize uncommonly, but regularly, with Rose-breasted Grosbeaks where their ranges meet in the Great Plains.

References   Hill (1995), Morlan (1991), Sibley (2000).

15.1 Definitive Alternate male Black-headed Grosbeak *Pheucticus melanocephalus*, Riverside County, California, USA, May 1997. In size and structure like Rose-breasted Grosbeak. Velvety black hood and upperparts contrast with uniform burnt orange collar, breast, and flanks. Belly yellow, blending to white undertail coverts. Wings with bold white spots on coverts and tertials (Brian E. Small).

15.2 Definitive Alternate male Black-headed Grosbeak *Pheucticus melanocephalus*, Riverside County, California, USA, April 2003. An unusual variant with a narrow, but conspicuous, complete white eye ring. Note yellow center to belly, white undertail coverts, and large white spots on underside of tail (Larry Sansone).

15.3 Female Black-headed Grosbeak *Pheucticus melanocephalus*, Riverside County, California, USA, April 1998. Similar to female Rose-breasted Grosbeak, but with rich buffy orange collar, throat, and breast with very fine streaking restricted to sides of breast and along flanks. Bold supercilium tinged buff. Bill is distinctly bicolored, with darker upper mandible (Brian E. Small).

15.4 Female Black-headed Grosbeak *Pheucticus melanocephalus*, Mount Pinos, California, USA, July 1995. By midsummer, breeding birds can appear very worn. On this bird note the much reduced wing bars and faded, paler color on breast (Brian E. Small).

15.5 First Alternate male Black-headed Grosbeak *Pheucticus melanocephalus*, southern California, USA, May 1995. Like adult male, but with worn brown primary coverts and flight feathers contrasting with black wing coverts and tertials. Often, as here, the black hood is broken up by a buffy orange supercilium (Herbert Clarke).

15.6 Female Black-headed Grosbeak *Pheucticus melanocephalus*, Willow Creek, New Mexico, USA, August 1994. Similar to spring female but slightly buffier on upperparts and with buff-tinged spots on wing coverts and tertials (Rick and Nora Bowers).

15.7 First Basic male Black-headed Grosbeak *Pheucticus melanocephalus,* Tucson, Arizona, USA, August 1993. Similar to adult female, but with uniform deep orange collar, throat, and breast. Head pattern more strikingly black and white. Best distinguished from Rose-breasted Grosbeak by unstreaked underparts and darker upper mandible. If visible, the underwing coverts on male Black-headed Grosbeaks are bright lemon yellow (Rick and Nora Bowers).

15a.1 Definitive Alternate male hybrid Rose-breasted ? Black-headed Grosbeak *Pheucticus ludovicianus* ? *melanocephalus,* Sawyer, North Dakota, USA, July 2004. This is a fairly typical individual showing mixed characters of both parent species. Rather similar to an adult male Black-headed Grosbeak, but with mostly whitish underparts contrasting with wide orange breast band. Center of the breast shows the inverted triangle of red typical of the male Rose-breasted Grosbeak. Bill appears to be uniformly pale gray, again more typical of Rose-breasted Grosbeak (Ron Martin).

16 Blue Bunting

(Cyanocompsa parellina)

Measurements
Length: 13.0–15.0 cm; 5.0–6 in.
Wing: 76–82 mm; 3.0–3.2 in.
Mass: 32.5 g.

The Blue Bunting is a causal winter visitor north of Mexico; since 1980, there have been thirty records from southern Texas, mostly from the Lower Rio Grande Valley (esp. Hidalgo County), including several in the winter of 2004–2005, and one record from southern Louisiana.

Habitat Blue Buntings are found in brushy forests and woodland edges, lowland evergreen forest edges, and pine-oak forest.

Behavior Blue Buntings tend to skulk in dense shrubs and can be difficult to see. Records from the United States are generally of single birds.

Voice The song is a sweet warble of clear phrases, starting with a couple of isolated notes, followed by variable jumbled phrases. The call is a simple, metallic *chip*.

Similar species The adult male resembles the adult male Indigo Bunting but is darker, with a darker bill and legs. The curved culmen is unlike that of *Passerina* buntings, and it is also somewhat thicker. The round tail differs from that of the *Passerina* buntings. The female is a richer, darker brown than the female Indigo Bunting, with no hint of streaking.

Geographic variation Three subspecies have been recognized. *C. p. lucida* is the form that doubtless is found casually north of Mexico.

Distribution *Resident* from central Sinaloa, e San Luis Potosí, n. Nuevo León, and central Tamaulipas south, locally, along both slopes of Central America, including the Yucatán Peninsula, to n-central Nicaragua.

    Casual to coastal s Texas (wintering in Hidalgo County; recently they have been seen more often than in the past) north to Brazoria County on the upper coast and to sw Louisiana (Cameron Parish).

Conservation status Extralimital in our area.

Molt Not described.

Description **Adult males**—Overall, very dark blue, with lighter blue highlights on the crown, malar area, lesser and median coverts, and rump. **Adult females**—Overall rich reddish brown, with primaries and rectrices darker; unstreaked. *Bill* black (males) or dark gray (females); *legs* and *feet* black.

Hybrids None reported.

References Dunn et al. (2002), Lockwood and Freeman (2004), Sibley (2000).

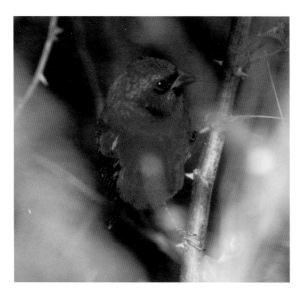

16.1 Male Blue Bunting *Cyanocompsa parellina*, Santa Anna National Wildlife Refuge, Texas, USA, December 1987. A smallish, stocky bunting with a rounded tail and stout bill. Overall dark blue, with shiny silvery blue highlights on supercilium and malar area. Note small blackish mask. Best distinguished from similar male Indigo Bunting by bill shape, black lores, and bright blue highlights on head (Mike Danzenbaker).

16.2 Female Blue Bunting *Cyanocompsa parellina*, Bentsen, Texas, USA, December 2000. Overall uniform brown. Beady black eye stands out on plain face. Bill and legs dusky gray. Similar to female Indigo Bunting but note more uniform chestnut brown plumage, dark bill with curved culmen, and rounded tail shape (Michael D. Stubblefield).

17 Blue Grosbeak

(Passerina caerulea)

Measurements
Length: 16.5–17.5 cm; 6.5–7.0 in.
Wing: 79–99 mm; 3.1–3.9 in. (sexes similar in size).
Mass: Male av. 29.3 g (27.1–31.4 g, $n = 10$); female av. 27.5 g (26.1–29.8 g, $n = 5$) (North Carolina).

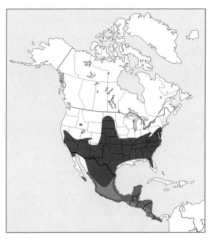

The Blue Grosbeak is a large *Passerina* bunting, and although it is significantly larger and heavier billed than the other *Passerina*, recently published molecular evidence shows that it is closely related to them. In the field, Blue Grosbeaks often show a slight crest. Like all members of that genus, they are strikingly sexually dimorphic in plumage coloration. Although nowhere particularly common, they are widespread, found from coast to coast, mostly in the southern United States.

Habitat During both summer and winter, Blue Grosbeaks are found in bushy, weedy fields, young deciduous second growth, and riparian thickets. In Sonora they are found up to 1600 m and are most common where cottonwoods, mesquite, and willows are all present. In migration and winter, they are sometimes found in cultivated fields, open grasslands, lawns, and other open areas. They sometimes forage with Indigo Buntings.

Behavior Tail flicking and spreading is common in Blue Grosbeaks—a characteristic behavior of *Passerina* buntings. In fall migration, they may gather in flocks in rice and grain fields, but during the breeding season they are territorial. Their walk has been described as "awkward."

Voice The song of the Blue Grosbeak is a rambling, rich, run-on warble that reminds one of a *Carpodacus* finch, but it lacks the burry quality of Purple and House finches and the paired phrases of Indigo Buntings. The call is a loud, metallic *tink* or *pink*.

Similar species Blue Grosbeaks superficially resemble the closely related Indigo Bunting but are larger, with a large head and bill. Individuals of both sexes have cinnamon or rufous wing bars—especially evident on males.

Geographic variation Four subspecies occur north of Mexico, one only as a vagrant. They show moderate geographic variation but are clinal where subspecies' ranges meet, and there is substantial within-group variation. *P. c. caerulea*, which occurs from the Great Plains eastward, is the smallest of the subspecies; it has a medium-size bill and is medium dark blue; females and first-year birds have medium brown up-perparts. *P. c. eurhyncha* is principally a Mexican race that is rare or vagrant in south-western Texas. It is the largest of the subspecies, with a large bill, and the Definitive Basic male is dark purplish blue. *P. c. interfusa* breeds from the central Great Plains west to east-central California. It is of medium size with a medium-size bill, and females and first-year birds are somewhat paler than eastern *P. c. caerulea*; their rump is gray-ish. *P. c. salicaria* breeds in the Southwest. It is of medium size and has a small bill. Males are medium blue, and females and first-year birds are pale medium brown.

Distribution   *Breeds* from n California, w and s Nevada, s Idaho (rare and irregu-lar), s-central Montana (rare), s-central North Dakota, sw Minnesota, central and ne Illinois, nw Indiana, n Ohio, s Pennsylvania, and se New York south to Georgia (lower elevations) and central Florida, rarely south to n Baja California and s Arizona, and in the highlands and Pacific lowlands of Central America through Mexico, Guatemala, El Salvador, Honduras, and Nicaragua to central Costa Rica and to s Tamaulipas, the coast of the Gulf of Mexico, and central Florida (and casually to s Florida). Reported in June east to Massachusetts.

Winters from s Baja California and n Mexico, s and the Gulf Coast of Florida (rare), and casually elsewhere in North America north to New England, and south through Central America to central Panama.

Migrates through most of Central America and across the Gulf of Mexico and is re-ported in the Bahamas, the Greater Antilles, the Cayman and Swan islands, and Bermuda.

Casual or rare north to Oregon, se British Columbia, s Saskatchewan, Wisconsin, central Ontario, s Quebec, New Brunswick, Nova Scotia, and Newfoundland; scarce but regular in fall in Atlantic Canada and New England. Accidental in Alaska (Peters-burg), e Ecuador, and Norway (June and November).

Conservation status   Although nowhere common, Blue Grosbeaks are stable in numbers, and they probably have benefited from the abandonment of marginal farms and (in the Southwest) from irrigation.

Molt   The brown Juvenal plumage is replaced by a Presupplemental molt during which all of the body plumage and most or all of the flight feathers are replaced; young males vary from being completely brown like females to mostly blue. The First Basic plumage is acquired by a Prebasic molt from July through October of most or all of the body plumage. The First Alternate plumage is acquired by a partial Prealternate molt in early spring, involving mostly head feathers. The Definitive Basic molt is com-plete and may be suspended during fall migration, and the Definitive Alternate plum-age is obtained by a limited Prealternate molt.

Description   **Adult males**—Bright blue with black face and lores and two bold ru-fous wing bars; the tips of feathers in fresh Basic males are buff or rusty, obscuring the blue color, which is exposed by wear; there is a lot of brown, especially on the mantle and *underparts*, on First Alternate (first-summer) males. **Adult females**—Brown, sometimes with blue flecks, with pale lores and undertail coverts and rusty median median coverts and buffy-tipped greater coverts, forming two wing bars. *Bill*, upper mandible black and lower mandible silver in males to brown in females; *legs* and *feet* pale brown; *iris* brown.

Hybrids   None described.

References   Ingold (1993), Pyle (1997), Russell and Monson (1998), Sibley (2003).

17.1 Definitive Alternate male Blue Grosbeak *Passerina caerulea*, Dry Tortugas, Florida, USA, April 1999. Larger and longer tailed than other *Passerina* buntings, with large, deep-based bill and slightly peaked crown. Overall bright blue, with black lores. Bright chestnut median coverts and tips to greater coverts form two distinct and rather wide wing bars. Large, steel gray bill (Kevin T. Karlson).

17.2 Definitive Alternate male Blue Grosbeak *Passerina caerulea*, Galveston, Texas, USA, April 2003. In fresh plumage the head and body feathers are tipped buff or brown; by spring they have abraded to leave a uniform blue appearance. This early spring bird still shows some very narrow brown fringing on the head, mantle, and underparts (Brian E. Small).

17.3 Female Blue Grosbeak *Passerina caerulea*, Riverside County, California, USA, May 2001. Overall grayish brown, with paler underparts. Buffy tips to median and greater coverts form two distinct wing bars. Can be confused with female Indigo Bunting but is larger and longer tailed, with deeper-based bill and usually obvious wing bars (Larry Sansone).

17.4 Female Blue Grosbeak *Passerina caerulea*, Galveston, Texas, USA, May 2000. Mostly grayish brown, buffy on face and breast, with whitish belly. Rump and tail dull blue. Note also blue-tinged lesser coverts and pale rufous tips to median and greater coverts. Female Lazuli Bunting also shows pale wing bars but is smaller, with a slighter bill (Brian E. Small).

17.5 First Alternate male Blue Grosbeak *Passerina caerulea*, Galveston, Texas, USA, April 2002. Highly variable, although this individual is fairly typical. Patchy blue and brown feathers on head and body, with blue-edged tail feathers. Bright chestnut wing bars are obvious. Best distinguished from non-breeding male Indigo Bunting by larger size, more massive bill, and obvious black on lores and around base of bill (Brian E. Small).

18 Lazuli Bunting

(Passerina amoena)

Measurements
Length: 13.0–14.0 cm; 5.0–5.5 in.
Wing: 64–77 mm (sexes similar in size).
Mass: Male av. 16.0 g (13.0–19.5 g,
  n = 58); female av. 15.0 g
  (12.7–16.9 g, n = 25) (California).

This colorful bunting is common in the western United States and southwestern Canada. A persistent singer, it is generally conspicuous throughout the spring and summer. The Lazuli Bunting is replaced in the east by the closely related Indigo Bunting; these species hybridize in the central Great Plains where their ranges meet.

Habitat   Lazuli Buntings are found in dry brushy areas, often near water, in riparian thickets, chaparral, and scrub oak, and are often abundant in recently burned chaparral. In winter, they frequently are found in loose flocks, often with other seed-eating birds, in open weedy areas and commonly in riparian areas, where sometimes they can be found in large numbers.

Behavior   Male Lazuli Buntings characteristically advertise their territories by singing from an exposed perch, generally in a tree. In summer, they eat many insects, some of which they pick while hovering. In migration and winter they are often found in small flocks, either of single- or mixed-species composition, and eat a mixed diet of seeds (which they sometimes obtain by bending down grasses) and insects. They are nocturnal migrants. Their flight is direct or slightly undulating, and they hop on the ground.

Voice   Their song is a complex, ordered sequence of elements, each usually repeated two to five times, and often very like the song of the Indigo Bunting. In general, their notes are less paired than in the song of the Indigo Bunting, but there is much overlap. Although individual males, after their first spring, sing an invariable song, there is a great deal of song variation in the species. First-spring males may mimic songs of older individuals, and thus there is a tendency for there to be local song dialects. Their most common call is a short *pit*, and a buzzy flight call is commonly heard.

Similar species   Adult males, with their orange breast and two bold wing bars, are unmistakable. Females resemble female Indigo Buntings but are paler in color with two buffy wing bars, and their undersides are unstreaked (although sometimes the juvenal streaking is retained in the Lazuli Bunting). Female Indigo and Varied buntings lack distinct wing bars, and the former are faintly streaked below. Female Painted Buntings are greenish and lack wing bars.

Geographic variation   No subspecies are recognized.

Distribution   *Breeds* from s-central British Columbia, s Alberta, s Saskatchewan, central North Dakota, and ne South Dakota south to nw Baja California, s California, s Nevada, central Arizona, central New Mexico, and central Texas, and east to w Nebraska, w Kansas, and w Oklahoma.

Winters from s Arizona and Chihuahua (casually north to central California and extreme w Texas) south to n Guerrero, central Veracruz, Puebla, and rarely to central Oaxaca.

Migrates through sw United States and nw Mexico, rarely west to sw British Columbia, central Alberta, and east to e and s Texas.

Casual in e North America (Manitoba, Minnesota, Wisconsin, Missouri, Illinois, Louisiana, Ontario, Pennsylvania, Maine, Maryland, South Carolina, and Florida). Accidental in s Mackenzie, se Alaska, and the Faeroes (one record, June).

Conservation status   Lazuli Buntings are generally common in suitable habitat. They are captured as cage birds in winter, but this probably has no significant impact on their populations.

Molt   In addition to a Prejuvenal molt, first-year Lazuli Buntings undergo three additional molts before their first breeding season. The first, a Presupplemental molt, involves only body feathers and takes place on the breeding ground. The First Prebasic molt takes place mostly at a couple of stopover points on migration, in southeastern Arizona and southwestern New Mexico, or in southern Baja California; it involves all body feathers and some remiges and coverts. The First Prealternate molt takes place on the wintering grounds, in winter and early spring; this molt is limited and involves mostly feathers around the eyes and bill. The Definitive Prebasic molt is complete; it begins on the breeding grounds but is interrupted for migration and completed at migratory stopover points. The Definitive Alternate plumage is acquired almost entirely by wear.

Description   Adult males—*Head*, mantle, and *rump* bright lazuli blue; lores dull black; median coverts broadly tipped in white, forming a broad wing bar; greater coverts narrowly tipped in white. Breast orange and flanks pale orange; otherwise *underparts* white. In fresh Basic plumage, (October through December) the feathers are tipped with brown, obscuring much of the blue, which is exposed as the feathers wear. In First Alternate plumage, some primary coverts and outer primaries and secondaries are dusky with bluish edgings, and the amount of blue and red in the plumage, especially in the *head* and throat region, is increased, in part by a limited molt and in part by wear. **Adult females**—Light brown to gray brown, often with an orange buff wash to the breast, and two indistinct wing bars. **First-winter** birds like females. *Bill*, upper mandible black, lower mandible light blue; *legs* and *feet* dark brown or black; *iris* black.

Hybrids   Lazuli Buntings hybridize regularly with Indigo where their ranges meet, especially in western Nebraska (along the Platte and Niobrara rivers), central South Dakota (along the Missouri River), and north-central North Dakota (along the Souris River).

References   Greene et al. (1996), Rising (1983).

18.1 Definitive Alternate male Lazuli Bunting *Passerina amoena*, Kern County, California, USA, June 2003. A small, compact *Passerina* bunting with a rather small bill. Virtually unmistakable, with bright blue head and upperparts, black lores, and wide orange breast band. Remaining underparts white, with pale orange flanks. Wings show two conspicuous white wing bars (Brian E. Small).

18.2 Definitive Alternate male Lazuli Bunting *Passerina amoena*, Kern County, California, USA, June 2003. The wide, sharply demarcated orange breast band is conspicuous in this front view. The belly and undertail coverts are white, with a buffy suffusion along flanks. This pattern is unique among *Passerina* buntings (Brian E. Small).

18.3 Female Lazuli Bunting *Passerina amoena*, Riverside County, California, USA, April 1996. Overall dull brown on upperparts, with dull blue wash on rump and tail. Underparts mostly whitish, with warmer buff breast and flanks. All wing feathers uniformly fresh, with blackish, blue-edged primary coverts indicating this is an adult bird. Best distinguished from female Indigo Bunting by narrow, pale wing bars and unstreaked, buffy orange breast. Could be confused with female Blue Grosbeak but is smaller and shorter tailed, with much smaller bill (Brian E. Small).

18.4 First Alternate male Lazuli Bunting *Passerina amoena*, Riverside County, California, USA, April 2002. Nonbreeding and First Alternate males show variable amount of patchy blue and brown on head and upperparts. The orange breast band is still conspicuous, though somewhat paler and less sharply demarcated than on breeding birds. This individual can be aged as a second-year bird because of the contrast between the fresh, blue-edged outer primary coverts and the retained Juvenal brown inner primary coverts (Brian E. Small).

18.5 Female Lazuli Bunting *Passerina amoena*, Riverside County, California, USA, May 1999. This bird shows obvious contrast between the retained worn and brownish primary coverts and the fresh, blackish-centered greater coverts. Some of the outer secondaries appear to be brown edged, and there is little blue on the lesser coverts and rump. These are all features of a second-year (First Alternate) female, but caution is advised in field conditions (Larry Sansone).

18.6 First Basic Lazuli Bunting *Passerina amoena*, Kern County, California, USA, October 2000. Similar to adult female but shows off-white underparts, with patchy buffy orange feathers on breast. Wings dusky, with sharply demarcated whitish tips to median and greater coverts. Best distinguished from the similar Indigo Bunting by grayer upperparts, some pale orange feathers on breast, and sharper wing bars (Brian E. Small).

18.7 Juvenile Lazuli Bunting *Passerina amoena*, Cabin Lake, Oregon, USA, August 1998. Similar to adult female but buffier overall, with some faint dusky streaking evident on buff-tinged breast and along flanks. Bill pinkish orange at base (Brian E. Small).

19 Indigo Bunting

(Passerina cyanea)

Measurements
Length: 12–14.5 cm; 5.0–6.0 in.
Wing: 60–72 mm; 2.4–2.8 in. (sexes similar in size).
Mass: Male av. 14.9 g (12.3–21.4 g, $n = 464$); female av. 14.1 g (11.2–18.6 g, $n = 339$) (Pennsylvania).

The Indigo Bunting is one of the most familiar and best-known American songbirds. Not only its breeding biology but also its migratory orientation and song development have they been the subjects of careful studies. Sexually dimorphic in color, adult males are bright indigo blue, whereas females are brownish. Males in their first summer are brownish but variably mottled with blue, especially around the head.

Habitat   Indigo Buntings breed in deciduous woodland edges, open woods, shrubby second growth, and riparian thickets. In migration and winter, they are found in a variety of semiopen scrubby and weedy habitats; they may occur singly or in flocks that can be rather large, and are often found with other seed-eating birds.

Behavior   Breeding males are highly territorial, often advertising their presence by singing persistently from an exposed perch. Males do not brood and usually do not associate with females at nests. In migration and winter they commonly are gregarious, and immatures often flock together on their breeding grounds, sometimes accompanied by adults. Indigo Buntings hop on the ground, and their flight is direct.

Voice   The songs of the Indigo Bunting are complex ordered sequences of several notes, often given in pairs, for example *ti ti whee whee zerre zerre*. Only males sing, and each male has a single complex song that it tends to retain throughout its life. Within the species, the song is highly variable, and a repertoire of about a hundred notes or "song figures" has been described from one population in Michigan. Indigo Buntings sometimes mimic the song of other species of birds. The call is a dry *spik*, *chip*, or *tink*. They have a buzzy flight note.

Similar species   The all-blue males are reasonably distinctive. Their small size and reasonably thin, finch-like bill distinguish them from the larger Blue Grosbeak, which has a much larger bill and two conspicuous rufous wing bars. Blue Bunting males are very dark blue in color and have a stouter bill than Indigo Buntings. Female Indigo Buntings are light buffy brown, usually with indistinct wing bars and a faintly streaked breast. Female Blue Buntings are a uniform dark ruddy brown and are unstreaked below.

Female Blue Grosbeaks are larger, with a rusty wing bar and a heavy bill. Female Lazuli Buntings are similar to female Indigo Buntings, but their wing bars usually are more distinct and their underparts are an unstreaked warm buff. Female Varied Buntings lack wing bars and are an unstreaked drab pale brown. Female Painted Buntings are decidedly greenish, often bright greenish in color, and their culmen is more curved.

Geographic variation   No subspecies are recognized.

Distribution   *Breeds* from se British Columbia, se Saskatchewan, s Manitoba, n Minnesota, s-central Ontario, s-central Quebec (Ottawa Valley, north to Manjwaki and upper St. Lawrence east to La Pocatière), s Maine, New Brunswick (rare), and w Nova Scotia (rare) south to Massachusetts (absent from Nantucket Island), s New Mexico, Texas (west to Big Bend and south to San Patricio County; uncommon on the South Plain), the Gulf Coast, and central Florida, and west to Montana, e Colorado, w Kansas, and central New Mexico; breeds sporadically in Colorado, sw Utah, central and se Arizona, and s California (where Indigo Buntings are often paired with Lazuli Buntings).

Winters from Nayarit and San Luis Potosí (rarely north to s Texas, the Gulf Coast, and in Florida, and casually elsewhere in North America) south through Mexico and Central America to nw Colombia, and in the West Indies. Rare in winter north to New Brunswick, New York, and Michigan.

Migrates through the United States east of the Rockies and in Mexico west to central Sonora and s Baja California Sur, through Bermuda and the w Greater Antilles, rarely but regularly through California, Baja California, nw Mexico, s Arizona, and New Mexico, and casually elsewhere in the West.

Casual north to nw and s-central Alaska (Wainwright, Anchorage), n Manitoba, central Quebec, Prince Edward Island, and Newfoundland. Accidental in the Revillagigedo Islands Mexico, and in Iceland, Britain, Ireland, Netherlands, Denmark, Sweden, and Finland (some vagrant records may be of escaped cage birds).

Conservation status   Indigo Buntings are common throughout much of their range and thrive in old fields, along roadsides, and in woodland edges. On their tropical wintering grounds, they are sometimes killed for food or kept as cage birds.

Molt   The First Basic plumage is acquired by a Prebasic molt of all of the body feathers except for the primary coverts and sometimes remiges. The First Alternate plumage of males is acquired by a partial Alternate molt, leaving them variously mottled with blue feathers (first-summer males may be as much as 80% brownish); usually all greater coverts are brown. Females in Alternate plumage resemble those in Basic plumage. Males in Definitive Basic plumage are similar to those in First Basic plumage except that they have bluish-edged greater coverts and are variably bluish on other tracts; males in Definitive Alternate plumage are bright blue, with black lores and occasionally with some retained brownish feathers. Definitive Alternate females are similar to First Basic females.

Description   Adult males—Bright indigo blue, often darker on the *head*, with black lores. The tips of the feathers are brown in freshly molted individuals, giving them a mottled blue and brown appearance. **First-summer males** are mottled blue and brown. **Adult females**—Gray or buffy brown, with a whitish throat, two indistinct wing bars, and lightly streaked *underparts*; the *tail* is bluish. *Bill* of males in the breeding season is blackish with a blue gray lower mandible; first-year males retain a yellowish gape into their first spring; females' upper mandible is dark brown or blackish, with lower mandible horn color; *legs* and *feet* dull blue gray to blackish; *iris* dark brown.

Hybrids   Indigo Buntings hybridize with Lazuli Buntings in the central Great Plains (see the Lazuli account). A female Indigo was courted by a male Painted Bunting in Kentucky (Fulton) in June 2003.

References   Payne (1992), Sibley (2003).

19.1 Definitive Alternate male Indigo Bunting *Passerina cyanea*, Dry Tortugas, Florida, USA, April 1998. A smallish, compact bunting. Overall bright blue, with slightly darker, more indigo-colored head. Wing coverts, primary coverts, flight feathers, and tail dusky black, broadly edged blue. Best distinguished from male Blue Grosbeak by smaller size, less massive bill, lack of black lores, and obvious chestnut wing bars (Kevin T. Karlson).

19.2 Female Indigo Bunting *Passerina cyanea*, Starr County, Texas, USA, April 1995. Mostly dull brown on head and upperparts, paler and buffier on face and underparts. Often, as here, shows narrow, buffy brown wing bars, which are usually less distinct than on similar female Lazuli Bunting. Note whitish throat, contrasting with weak dusky submoustachial stripe. Shows some dull blue feathers on lesser coverts and rump, with blue edge to primary coverts and flight feathers (Greg W. Lasley).

19.3 Female Indigo Bunting *Passerina cyanea*, Dry Tortugas, Florida, May 1999. This bird shows contrast between worn and brown primary coverts and fresher, darker-centered greater coverts and is probably a second-year (First Alternate) individual. Similar to female Lazuli Bunting, but with less distinct wing bars, whiter throat, and some blurry, dusky streaking on breast and flanks (Kevin T. Karlson).

19.4 First Alternate male Indigo Bunting *Passerina cyanea*, Galveston, Texas, USA, April 2003. Nonbreeding and First Alternate males are highly variable, with a mix of brown and blue feathers on head, body, and wings. The retained brown primary coverts, wing coverts, and tertials indicate this bird is in its second calendar year. Most likely to be confused with larger Blue Grosbeak but note smaller bill, more rounded head shape, shorter tail, and less obvious rufous wing bars (Brian E. Small).

19.5 First Alternate male Indigo Bunting *Passerina cyanea*, Galveston, Texas, USA, April 2003. Like the bird in figure 19.4, this individual is in its second calendar year. The wing coverts and some of the tertials have been replaced, but the primary coverts, secondaries, and inner primaries are old and contrastingly brown (Brian E. Small).

19.6 Basic female Indigo Bunting *Passerina cyanea*, Tucson, Arizona, USA, January 1991. Similar to Alternate female but warmer brown on upperparts and extensively buffy cinnamon on underparts. Rather like the nonbreeding female Lazuli Bunting but note whitish throat, blurry streaks on breast, and less distinct, brownish wing bars (Rick and Nora Bowers).

19.7 First Basic Indigo Bunting *Passerina cyanea*, Marana, Arizona, USA, September 1994. Similar to nonbreeding female, but with more distinct dusky streaking across breast and along flanks. Bill and gape mostly pinkish orange (Rick and Nora Bowers).

2 0 **Varied Bunting**

(Passerina versicolor)

Measurements
Length: 11.5–12.5 cm; 4.5–5.0 in.
Wing: 58–72 mm; 2.3–2.8 in. (sexes similar in size).
Mass: 11.8 g (Sinaloa, Mexico).

Although the Varied Bunting is widespread and often observed in central Mexico, little is known of its biology. Males are quite colorful but can appear to be black in poor light.

Habitat Varied Buntings are found in dry scrub, frequently on arid hillsides, in riparian thickets, and in overgrown clearings. In winter they may be found singly or in small groups, and may move to less arid habitats.

Behavior In the northern parts of their range, where they are migratory, males arrive before females and establish territories by singing and by chasing other males. Individuals of both sexes may return to the same territory that they occupied in previous years. During migration they may be found in flocks, sometimes rather large flocks. They forage on the ground or in shrubs and small trees, and hop on the ground and on the branches of shrubs and small trees.

Voice The song consists of several syllables, which are rarely paired. Only males sing. Adult males sing an invariable song, although there is considerable interindividual variation. Songs are said to be somewhat lower and harsher than those of other *Passerina* buntings. First-year males may incorporate syllables from other males into their songs. Within an area, males may countersing. The calls are *buzz* and *chip* notes.

Similar species Adult males are distinctive but, if not seen well or in sunlight, can appear to be nearly black; this is particularly true for birds from Texas, which are not as brightly colored as those from farther west. Females are uniformly brown in color and resemble female Indigo Buntings (which are, however, faintly streaked ventrally) and female Lazuli Buntings (which have distinct wing bars). The curved culmen of Varied Buntings is distinctive. Female Blue Buntings are a darker, richer reddish brown in color and have a short, stout bill.

Geographic variation Two subspecies of Varied Buntings have been described from our area, *P. v. dickeyae*, which occurs in southern Arizona and New Mexico south to Jalisco and Colima, and *P. v. versicolor*, which occurs from southern and western Texas south to central Veracruz, central Oaxaca, and Guerrero. The plumage of female and young birds of the former averages more reddish than that of the latter, which is grayish brown. The throat of adult male *P. v. dickeyae* is purple and the nape bright red, whereas the nape of *P. v. versicolor* is a dull red and the throat reddish purple. Birds from southern Arizona are slightly larger than those from Sonora.

Distribution   *Resident* from s Baja California, n Sonora, s-central and se Arizona, s New Mexico, and w and s Texas (Culberson and Crockett counties, and the Rio Grande Valley) south through Mexico (except for the Yucatán Peninsula) to central Oaxaca and in central Chiapas and e-central Guatemala. Withdraws from the northern part of its range in winter.
   Casual in se California; accidental in Ontario (Long Point).

Conservation status   Much of the habitat that Varied Buntings used to occupy in southern Texas has been converted into agricultural land, and in New Mexico (where they are very local) the species is listed as threatened. They are commonly kept as caged birds in Mexico.

Molt   In first-year birds there is a partial Presupplemental molt that takes place from early July through September; this involves some or all of the body plumage except for the greater primary coverts and secondary coverts. The First Prebasic molt is partial and includes most or all of the body plumage and usually all of the rectrices, several inner secondaries, and outer primaries; this occurs in fall and winter and may not be complete until mid-January. There is a partial First Prelaternate molt that takes place in winter and especially in April. The Definitive Prebasic molt is complete, and there is a limited Definitive Prealternate molt.

Description   Adult males—Lower forehead, lores, and chin black; face, *rump*, and undertail coverts dark blue; posterior part of the crown, nape, and neck dark red (not always obvious), and posterior margin of the eye with a bright red eye ring; *underparts* dull violet, becoming blue posteriorially. In fresh Basic birds, the feathers are extensively tipped with brown. **Adult females**—Uniformly dull brown, somewhat paler below; undertail coverts are pale beige, and worn birds are more pallid than those in fresh plumage. **Young** resemble adult females. *Bill*, upper mandible black or blackish brown, lower mandible paler, light brownish or pale bluish; the culmen is decurved; *legs* and *feet* purplish gray; *iris* dark brown.

Hybrids   Varied Buntings have hybridized with Painted Buntings.

Reference   Groschupf and Thompson (1998).

20.1 Definitive Alternate male Varied Bunting *Passerina versicolor*, Crockett County, Texas, USA, June 2000. A smallish, compact bunting with noticeably curved culmen. Virtually unmistakable, with rich, dark plumage. Mostly purplish blue, with pinkish suffusion on mantle and breast. Nape bright red and lores contrastingly black (Greg W. Lasley).

20.2 Definitive Alternate male Varied Bunting *Passerina versicolor*, Crockett County, Texas, USA, June 2000. In this back view note the contrast between the shining blue rump and the brownish purple mantle. The bright red nape and eye crescents stand out on the otherwise blue and black head (Greg W. Lasley).

20.3 Female Varied Bunting *Passerina versicolor*, Arivaca Creek, Arizona, USA, June 2003. Rather drab. Best distinguished from other female *Passerina* buntings by more uniform, colder grayish brown overall appearance and more curved culmen on bill. Rump, tail, and lesser coverts are washed with dull blue. Head rather plain but note buffy eye ring and paler throat (Jim Burns/Natural Impacts).

20.4 Basic female Varied Bunting *Passerina versicolor*, Alamosa, Sonora, Mexico, January 1996. Very much like breeding female but in fresh plumage, as here, can appear more warmish brown, lacking gray tones often present on worn summer birds. Wing coverts show cinnamon brown tips, forming very obscure wing bars. Could be confused with a female Blue Bunting but note bill color and shape, paler underparts, and blue-edged tail feathers (Rick and Nora Bowers).

20.5 Basic male Varied Bunting *Passerina versicolor*, Madera Canyon, Arizona, USA, September 1993. Similar to breeding male, but with buffy brown fringes to head and body feathers. Note the red eye crescents and black lores and area around bill. This bird is in active wing molt and has yet to replace the worn and rather brown-looking outer primaries (Rick and Nora Bowers).

2 1 **Painted Bunting**

(Passerina ciris)

Measurements
Length: 12–13 cm; ca. 5 in.
Wing: 58–72 mm; 2.3–2.8 in. (sexes similar in size).
Mass: Male av. 16.1 g (13.3–19.0 g, $n = 116$); female av. 15.0 g (12.9–19.0 g, $n = 131$) (Florida).

The adult male Painted Bunting, with his red underparts and rump, bright green back, and blue head, is unquestionably one of the most colorful and distinctive North American birds. The female, although subtle in coloration, is also quite distinctive—the only finch-like bird that is uniformly greenish.

Habitat   Painted Buntings are found in dense brush with scattered trees and in humid riparian thickets. Along the southern Atlantic coast, they are found in coastal thickets. In winter they may be found in arid thorn forests or humid thickets; they often feed with other seed-eating birds.

Behavior   Territorial males advertise their territories by singing from a conspicuous perch. In spring male-male fighting is fairly common as they are establishing breeding territories. During courtship, the males can show a *bow display*, during which the male faces a conspecific, bows his head, and raises his tail. They also perform a *butterfly flight*, characterized by slow, deep wing beats, and a *moth flight*, which is a slow, descending flight. They are nocturnal migrants and often are found in small, loose flocks, often with Indigo Buntings. On the ground, they usually hop, but may walk during some displays.

Voice   Only males sing, and the song is sweet; it is continuous like that of the Indigo Bunting but more musical, and lacking the repeated elements. It has been described as a *witee wiwitee wita witato*, or *tida dayda tidayday teetayta totah*. The call note is *pik-pik-pik*, or a single *plick, pit,* or *pitch*.

Similar species   Both sexes are unmistakable. Although the female is dull in coloration, this is the only species of finch-like bird with an all-green plumage; other female *Passerina* are brownish.

Geographic variation   Two subspecies of Painted Buntings are recognized, *P. c. ciris*, which breeds in the southeastern United States, from southern Missouri east through Tennessee to North Carolina and south to eastern Texas, and *P. c. pallidior*, which breeds from southeastern New Mexico and southern Kansas south through central and western Texas to southern Chihuahua, northern Coahuila, and southern Texas. The western birds average larger and paler than the eastern birds, but the variation is clinal, and differences are obscured by individual variation. Many workers do not recognize these races.

Distribution   *Breeds* from se New Mexico, n Texas, w and central Oklahoma, w-central Kansas, s Missouri, and sw Tennessee south to s Chihuahua, n Coahuila, s Texas, and s Louisiana, and east along the Gulf Coast to s Alabama, and from central South Carolina and se North Carolina south, primarily on barrier islands and the adjacent mainland coast, to central Florida. Reported in May in Saskatchewan, Ohio, Maine, and s Quebec, and June in w Ontario (Old Fort William).

   Winters from Sinaloa, s Tamaulipas, s Florida, coastal North Carolina (few), and nw Bahama Islands south through Cuba, Jamaica, and Central America (both slopes) to w Panama, casually north to s Arizona and w and s Texas.

   Migrates west rarely to s California and Arizona.

   Casual north, especially in the fall, in Massachusetts, Minnesota, Wisconsin, Michigan, Pennsylvania, Ontario, New Brunswick (mostly May and June), and Nova Scotia, west to Washington (Seattle), se Wyoming, Oregon, California, and Nevada, and on Bermuda (four records). Some extralimital records may be of escaped cage birds. There are six British records (April–July) that may be of wild birds; two records from Norway probably are of escapees.

Conservation status   These are popular cage birds and are easily caught, probably in sufficiently high numbers to affect their population size. In the southeastern United States, where their range is limited, Painted Buntings have declined in numbers, probably because of habitat degradation, which is probably the most significant cause of population declines. This species has been placed on a "watch list" as a species of special concern.

Molt   The Juvenal plumage is acquired by a complete Prejuvenal molt, mid-May through July. Supplemental plumage is acquired by an incomplete Presupplemental molt and typically involves most of the body plumage but not the greater primary or secondary coverts; this occurs June through October, usually on the breeding grounds. The First Basic plumage is acquired by a partial First Prebasic molt, September through November, and involves all rectrices, the outer primaries, and inner secondaries; birds that breed in the Southeast undergo this molt on the breeding grounds, but over half of the western birds go through this molt during migration in the southwestern United States or northwestern Mexico. The First Alternate plumage is partial; it includes the head and some body feathers and occurs on the wintering grounds, mid-December through mid-May. The Definitive Basic plumage is acquired by a complete Definitive Prebasic molt, mid-August through mid-October, and the Definitive Prealternate plumage is acquired by a partial molt that occurs January through May and involves head and some other body plumage.

Description   Adult males—Crown, nape, and sides of face bright dark blue, with a thin, bright red eye ring; *back* has a bright chartreuse or lime green mantle; *rump*, throat, and *underparts*, including undertail coverts and uppertail coverts, bright red; *wings* blackish with green edges to coverts, secondaries, and tertials; *tail* dark. Adult females—Uniformly lime greenish, with *head*, scapulars, and *tail* darker than *underparts*. First-year birds—Females like adult females but a duller green; males are variable but generally brighter, with a few scattered blue and red feathers in their plumage. **Bill** dark brown or blackish; **legs** and **feet** dark gray or dull dusky brown; **iris** dark brown.

Hybrids   Painted Buntings have hybridized with Varied Buntings. In Kentucky (Fulton) a male (the state's first record) courted a female Indigo Bunting in June 2003 but was not known to nest.

References   Lowther et al. (1999), Thompson (1991a, b).

21.1 Definitive Alternate male Painted Bunting *Passerina ciris*, Galveston, Texas, USA, April 2003. A smallish, compact *Passerina* bunting. The gaudy breeding male is unmistakable. The shining blue head contrasts with bright lime green mantle and gleaming red rump. The throat and underparts are uniform bright red. Note red eye crescents and black lores (Brian E. Small).

21.2 Female Painted Bunting *Passerina ciris*, Dry Tortugas, Florida, USA, May 1997. Differs from all other female *Passerina* buntings by bright grass green head and upperparts and dull buffy yellow underparts. Head rather plain apart from pale eye crescents. Wings lack any noticeable wing bars (Kevin T. Karlson).

21.3 First Alternate male Painted Bunting *Passerina ciris*, Galveston, Texas, USA, May 2000. Similar to female and likewise mostly greenish. This bird can confidently be sexed as a male by the blue feathers on the head. Note that the alulae, primary coverts, and inner primaries are contrastingly worn and brown, a feature typical of second-year birds (Brian E. Small).

21.4 First Basic male or female Painted Bunting *Passerina ciris*, Kern County, California, USA, October 2000. Like adult female but not so bright overall, especially on the underparts. The orange yellow gape suggests this is a First Basic bird and therefore cannot be reliably sexed at this time of year (Larry Sansone).

21.5 First Alternate male or female Painted Bunting *Passerina ciris*, Galveston, Texas, USA, May 2001. This individual shows obvious contrast between the retained worn and brownish primary coverts and the fresher blue-green-edged greater coverts and primaries. This bird is possibly a female, but the lack of any red or blue body feathers does not rule out a second-year male (see figure 21.3) (Brian E. Small).

21.6 Juvenile Painted Bunting *Passerina ciris*, Kino Springs, Arizona, USA, August 2001. Similar to breeding female but decidedly duller green on the head and upperparts, with dull, pale grayish buff underparts. Note obscure dusky streaking on breast and flanks and pale tips to wing coverts, forming narrow wing bars. Gape and base of lower mandible pale orange (Kevin T. Karlson).

2 2 Dickcissel

(Spiza americana)

Measurements
Length: 13.0–17.5 cm; 5.0–6.9 in.
Wing: Males 77–86 mm, 3.0–3.4 in.; females 69–78 mm, 2.7–3.1 in.
Mass: Male av. 29.3 g; female av. 24.6 g (Great Plains).

The Dickcissel is a typical and locally abundant breeding bird in North American tallgrass prairie, with its core breeding range in southern Iowa, eastern Kansas and Nebraska, and central Oklahoma, east to central Illinois. In the nineteenth century, it also bred along the eastern seaboard where people had created suitable habitat by clearing the forests. They are sparrow-like in appearance, and indeed the female resembles a female House Sparrow. Males, with black breast and yellow on the breast and around the eyes, look a bit like small, sparrow-like meadowlarks.

Habitat Dickcissels are found along roadsides in grasslands, tallgrass prairie, overgrown bushy fields, and in croplands, especially in alfalfa. In South America, in winter, they are found in cleared areas, llanos, and in croplands, especially rice fields. In winter, they occur singly or in flocks, sometimes large flocks.

Behavior Following the breeding season, Dickcissels form large flocks that move southward to their wintering grounds. Migration is principally at night, but large flocks can be seen during the day moving to foraging sites. In the breeding season, males are territorial, and territorial males chase intruding males. They advertise their territory by singing from a conspicuous perch and monotonously repeating their song. Female to female aggression has not been observed. Males with high-quality territories may obtain more than one mate. Dickcissels walk or hop on the ground.

Voice Their song is a characteristic *see see cikc-dick chee chee*, or *dick dick sic sic sic*, hence the name Dickcissel. The call, often given in flight, is a buzzy ("electric") *bzeet*.

Similar species Male Dickcissels are unmistakable, although they rather vaguely resemble small, finch-like meadowlarks. Females resemble female House Sparrows because of their size, dull coloration, and general structure, and, curiously, vagrant individuals may be found in flocks of House Sparrows.

Geographic variation None has been described.

Distribution *Breeds* from e Montana (west sporadically to Sheridan), s Saskatchewan, s Manitoba, w and s Minnesota (north to Cass, Polk, and Red Lake counties), n Wisconsin (sometimes locally common), n Michigan, s Ontario (rare and irregular), Indiana (locally common in some years), and central New York south to ne Wyoming, e Colorado, ne New Mexico (rare), w and s Texas, s Louisiana, central Mississippi, Alabama (rare in south), central and se Georgia (rare and irruptive), and South Carolina, and at least formerly also in the Atlantic lowlands from Massachusetts to North Carolina; breeding is sporadic in the East.

Winters from Nayarit south, primarily along the Pacific slope, through Central America to n and e Colombia, Venezuela (where abundant), Trinidad, and the Guianas, and locally in small numbers in coastal lowlands from s New England south to Florida and west to coastal and s Texas. In winter they are casual north to the Great Lakes region and northwest to e Colorado.

Migrates through e United States and Bahama Islands, through Central America (both slopes), and casually through California, central Baja California, s Arizona, e and s New Mexico, Cuba, Jamaica, Puerto Pico, the Cayman Islands, islands in the western Caribbean Sea, and the Netherlands Antilles.

Casual or scarce and irregular north to Alaska (Juneau, May), s British Columbia, s Alberta, s Quebec, s New Brunswick (sometimes through winter at feeders), Prince Edward Island, Nova Scotia, and Newfoundland, and south to central Baja California and to Bermuda and Clipperton Island; accidental in Norway.

Conservation status In winter, Dickcissels are widely hunted and eaten. In Venezuela, where they can be found in large flocks, they can be a significant pest on grain (especially rice) crops, and for this reason some farmers illegally poison them, often killing them in large numbers (one farmer acknowledged killing more than a million). Changes in their habitat—converting grasslands to croplands—in their core breeding area (in the central Great Plains) have resulted in population declines, and hay mowing often results in nest failure. Severe population declines from 1966 to 1978 resulted in their being listed as declining but not yet threatened. Recently, however, their numbers seem to have stabilized at about two-thirds of their numbers in 1966. During the nineteenth century, Dickcissels were a common breeding species in agricultural grasslands of eastern North America, from New England south through the Carolinas and occasionally north to maritime Canada, but this eastern area was largely abandoned by the end of the nineteenth century, no doubt because of the reversion of such grasslands to habitats no longer suitable to them.

Molt The Juvenal plumage is acquired by a complete Prejuvenal molt that takes place five to twenty days after hatching. The First Basic plumage is acquired by a partial First Prebasic molt that includes body feathers, median and greater wing coverts, and occasionally some tertials and the central rectrices. The First Alternate plumage is acquired by a partial molt, December to April, and includes body feathers and occasionally some median wing coverts. First Alternate males resemble Definitive Alternate males except that they retain some Juvenal feathers (alulae, primary coverts, remiges, and rectrices); First Alternate females resemble Definitive Alternate females except that some Juvenal feathers are retained. The Definitive Basic plumage is acquired by a complete Definitive Basic molt that occurs on the breeding grounds, June through October; the Definitive Alternate molt is like the First Alternate molt.

Description   Adult males—Forehead, malar, and supercilium yellow, with supercilium becoming whitish posterior to the eye; crown, ear coverts, hind neck, and nape gray; mantle brown, boldly streaked with dark brown; lower **back**, **rump**, and uppertail coverts grayish brown; throat whitish; upper breast black; lower breast washed with yellowish; belly and flanks brownish; undertail coverts whitish; lesser and median coverts bright rufous chestnut; greater coverts and tertials dark brown, edged in buff. **Adult females—Upperparts** and side of neck buff brown; forehead, malar, and supercilium washed with yellowish; mantle with dark brown streaks; **tail** brownish; throat whitish, laterally edged with dark brown; breast washed with yellowish; belly and flanks grayish; undertail coverts whitish; median coverts dull chestnut. **First-winter** resemble adult females but have little yellow on the breast and fine streaks on the breast and flanks. **Bill**, culmen slate black to black; lower mandible paler, tinged with bluish; in winter bill pale; **legs** and **feet** pale pinkish buff, becoming darker with age; **iris** dark brown.

Hybrids   There is a reported hybrid between a Dickcissel and a Blue Grosbeak that may simply be an aberrant Dickcissel. Audubon's "Townsend's Bunting," known only by the type specimen, may be an aberrant female Dickcissel.

Reference   Temple (2002).

22.1 Male Dickcissel *Spiza americana*, Galveston, Texas, USA, April 2001. Chunky and rather short tailed, with a deep-based, longish bill. Distinctive head pattern, with yellow patches on supercilium and malar, gray auriculars and crown, and black bar on lower throat. Underparts whitish, tinged buff on flanks, with bright yellow patch on breast. Upperparts similar to those of female House Sparrow *Passer domesticus*, but with obvious rufous shoulder patch (Brian E. Small).

22.2 Female Dickcissel *Spiza americana*, Dallas, Texas, USA, June 2001. Like a drab version of the male, with less contrasting head pattern and duller chestnut edges to median and lesser wing coverts. Yellow patch on breast paler and more diffuse, with some fine, dusky streaking. Dusky sub-moustachial stripe and spotted gorget across upper breast contrasts with white throat and malar (Rick and Nora Bowers).

22.3 First Basic female Dickcissel *Spiza americana*, Cape May, New Jersey, USA, October 2002. Rather drab and House Sparrow–like. Upperparts grayish brown, streaked with black, and showing distinct pale braces on mantle. Little or no rufous in wing coverts. Head shows thin, yellow-tinged supercilium and whitish lower eye crescent. Malar and throat white, contrasting with drab, finely streaked underparts (Kevin T. Karlson).

22.4 Female or First Basic male Dickcissel *Spiza americana*, Riverside County, California, USA, September 1994. A brighter fresh fall bird than the one shown in figure 22.3, with some yellow on supercilium, malar area, and breast. Aging and sexing of fall birds can be difficult, but the amount of yellow on the breast suggests an adult female or a First Basic male (Brian E. Small).

2 3 Common Chaffinch

(Fringilla coelebs)

Measurements
Length: 14.5 cm; 5.7 in.
Wing: 82–95 mm; 3.2–3.7 in.
Mass: 20–28 g (Norway).

A Eurasian species, the Common Chaffinch is accidental in eastern Canada and northeastern United States.

Habitat In Europe, Common Chaffinches are found in a variety of woodlands. In Scandinavia, highest densities are found in deciduous woods, but they also occur in spruce or pines. In North America, they should be looked for at feeders.

Behavior In Europe, Common Chaffinches occur in mixed flocks, but in North America single birds are seen. Chaffinches walk rather than hop, and have an undulating flight. Their foods are seeds, buds, fruit, spiders, and insects and their larvae.

Voice The song of the chaffinch is a descending, melodious rattle of several notes, followed by a rapid series of *chip* notes. The call is a distinctive metallic *chink*, given as a single or double note.

Similar species Unmistakable in our area.

Geographic variation In Eurasia, many different subspecies are recognized. Individuals reported in North America probably originated in northwestern Europe, where *F. c. coelebs* breeds.

Distribution *Breeds* in w Palearctic from Scandinavia south to North Africa and east to Lake Baikal.
   Winters from s Norway south to North Africa and sw Asia.
   Accidental in ne North America. A female photographed at Middle Cove, Newfoundland (21 May 1994), was found with an incursion of European vagrants. There are about twelve other records e Canada, New England, and New Jersey, reported between late September and late May. Reports of chaffinches from California, Wyoming, Indiana, Ohio, and Louisiana (December) are probably of escaped cage birds.

Conservation status The Chaffinch is extralimital in our area but is generally common—in some places abundant—in its Eurasian range.

Molt The prebasic molt is complete, starting (in Britain) in mid-June and completed by early October.

Description **Adult males**—Forehead blackish, merging to gray blue on crown, nape, and neck; sides of head, lores, anterior supercilium, and ear coverts and cheek pink, tinged with orange. Mantle reddish brown to chestnut, becoming blue green on scapulars; lower **back** and **rump** green or deep green, extending onto the upper coverts; **tail** black with slate gray center; outer rectrices white. **Wings** blackish with white median and outer lesser coverts; greater coverts black, broadly tipped with white; bases of innermost primaries white; leading edges of flight feathers white. **Adult females**—Patterned like males but without rich chestnut and gray colors: crown, supercilium, and nape pale gray, with a brownish lateral crown stripe and postocular stripe; *underparts* buffy gray. *Bill* blue gray (males) or brownish (females), darker at tip; *legs* and *feet* pinkish brown, duller in winter; *iris* black.

Hybrids   Wild hybrids with Brambling have been recorded. In captivity, they have been reported to have been crossed with Linnet (*Carduelis cannabina*), European Goldfinch (*C. carduelis*), Common Redpoll (*C. flammea*), Greenfinch (*C. chloris*), Canary (*Serinus serinus*), Eurasian Bullfinch (*Pyrrhula pyrrhula*), and House Sparrow (*Passer domesticus*). Most of these hybrids appear not to be viable.

References   Clement et al. (1993), Cramp and Perrins (1994a), Dunn et al. (2002), Gray (1958).

23.1 Male Common Chaffinch *Fringilla coelebs*, Oxon, UK, April 2003. A medium-size finch with peaked crown and longish, spike-like bill. Rather colorful with gray crown and nape, contrasting with rusty cinnamon face and pinkish breast. Brown mantle contrasts with green rump (not visible here). Wings are black, with conspicuous white wing bars and pale yellowish edges to flight feathers (George Reszeter).

23.2 Female Common Chaffinch *Fringilla coelebs*, Oxon, UK, September 2003. Much drabber than male, with brown upperparts and buffy gray face and breast. Buffy white wing bars and outer tail feathers less flashy than in male but still an obvious feature. Structure similar to Brambling's but much less colorful, lacking orange on wings and underparts (George Reszeter).

24 **Brambling**

(Fringilla montifringilla)

Measurements
Length: 14.5–18 cm; 5.7–7.1 in.
Wing: 84–97 mm; 3.3–3.8 in. (males larger than females; Scandinavia).
Mass: 17.0–34.9 g (males somewhat heavier than females).

Bramblings are unmistakable birds, which, within their Eurasian range, are often are found in large flocks in fall and winter. In North America, most records are of single birds.

Habitat Bramblings are found in mixed forest, forest edges, open birch woodlands, and riparian willows; in winter they are found in woodlands and weedy fields. In North America, they should be looked for at feeders.

Behavior In winter, Bramblings may be found in large flocks, although in North America only single birds are likely to be encountered. They feed on the ground, frequently flying up into nearby trees or shrubs; they have a strong, undulating flight.

Voice The song of the Brambling is described as being rather sweet and melodious, with flute-like notes and a descending musical rattle. The call is a sharp, rasping *zweee*.

Similar species Unmistakable in our area.

Geographic variation No geographic variation has been described.

Distribution *Breeds* from n Scandinavia, n Russia, and n Siberia south to s Scandinavia, central Russia, northern Amurland, Kamchatka, and the Sea of Okhotsk. There is one nesting record for Attu, Aleutian Islands.

Winters from the British Isles and s parts of the breeding range south to the Mediterranean region, n Africa and Near East, Iran, nw India, Tibet, China, Taiwan, and Japan.

Migrates regularly through the w and central Aleutian Islands (rare; in spring from 9 May to 22 June; in fall from mid-September to mid-October) and causally east in the Aleutians to Kasatochi Island (28 June) and the islands in the Bering Sea (St. Lawrence [June], St. Matthew Island [June], and St. Paul Island in the Pribilofs [October, June, July]), and through w (Hopper Bay [June]) and s-coastal (Cordova [November]) Alaska.

Casual in w North America from n (Barrow [September]) and se (Juneau [December]) Alaska, British Columbia, Oregon (fall and winter), central Alberta, Saskatchewan, Manitoba (six records, one from Winnipeg in May), Idaho (two records), Montana (Arlee), North Dakota (Bismark), and Minnesota south to central California, Nevada, n Utah, Colorado, and Kansas (Linn County, winter), and east to Michigan, Indiana, Ohio, Ontario (Atikokan), Quebec, Pennsylvania, New York, Massachusetts, New Jersey, and Nova Scotia.

Conservation status Bramblings are common or locally common, and there are signs that they are increasing their range toward both the north and the south, although long-term changes are not clear.

Molt   There is a partial First Basic molt involving head and body feathers, lesser and median coverts, and a variable number of greater coverts; this molt occurs in July and August. There is a complete Definitive Basic molt that occurs in July and August.

Description   **Adult males**—In fall, forehead, crown, and sides of nape grayish buff; center of nape pale grayish buff; mantle, *back*, and scapulars colored like forehead, but often more black visible; *rump* and uppertail coverts white; *tail* black; throat, breast, shoulder, and greater coverts orange; flanks orange with black spots; belly and undertail coverts white. Spring plumage acquired by wear: *head*, nape, *back*, and mantle black; otherwise like fall males. **Adult females**—Crown, sides of nape, and mantle brown and slightly mottled; ear coverts and center of nape pale buffy gray; *rump* and uppertail coverts white; *tail* brown; throat, breast, and scapulars pale buffy gray; belly whitish, with faint brown spotting on the flanks; undertail coverts white. **First-year birds** like adult females but duller, with a pale center to their crown. *Bill* of males in summer is bluish, tipped with black; bill of females pale yellowish or bluish, tipped with brown; *legs* and *feet* pale pinkish; *iris* dark brown.

Hybrids   Wild hybrids with Chaffinches have been reported, and in captivity they have been crossed with Linnets, Common Redpolls, European Greenfinches, Bullfinches, and Canaries. Most of these hybrids appear to be nonviable.

References   Clement et al. (1993), Cramp and Perrins (1994a), Gray (1958), Newton (1973), Winker et al. (2003).

24.1 Spring male Brambling *Fringilla montifringilla*, Attu Island, Alaska, USA, May 1999. A mediun-size finch with longish wings and tail. Distinctive combination of blackish head and upperparts and bright rusty orange breast and shoulder patch. Wings blackish, with wide orange bar on greater coverts. White rump (not visible here) obvious in flight. Bill black (Jim Burns/Natural Impacts).

24.2 Basic male Brambling *Fringilla montifringilla*, Japan, January 1999. Like spring male but head mostly gray, with brown wash on crown and auricular and darker lateral crown stripes. Snowy white underparts contrast with bright rusty orange throat, breast, and flanks. Bill mostly pinkish, with darker tip and culmen (Mike Danzenbaker).

24.3 Female Brambling *Fringilla montifringilla*, Attu Island, Alaska, USA, May 1999. Similar to basic male but paler overall, with buffy orange throat, breast, and flanks. Wings show pale orange shoulder patch and bar on greater coverts. Note long primary extension and rather peaked crown shape (Jim Burns/Natural Impacts).

24.4 Basic female Brambling *Fringilla montifringilla*, Japan, January 1999. Like basic male but paler gray on head, and with pale orange throat, breast, and flanks suffused with brown. Note the striking wing pattern, with long primary extension (Mike Danzenbaker).

2 5 Gray-crowned Rosy-Finch

(Leucosticte tephrocotis)

Measurements

Length: 14.0–18.0 cm; 5.5–7.1 in. (geographically variable).

Wing: 102–124 mm; 4.0–4.9 in. (males slightly larger than females; geographically variable).

Mass: Males 21.3–27.0 g, av. 24.1 g; females 21.6–29.4 g, av. 23.6 g (eastern California) Males 41.2–51.2 g, av. 45.3 g; females 42.1–59.9 g, av. 48.5 g (Aleutian Islands).

The Gray-crowned Rosy-Finch is the most widespread of the rosy-finches, breeding from Alaska south to western Montana and in the Sierra Nevada in east-central California. As with all rosy-finches, its English name derives from rosy underparts and rump. Both this species and the Black Rosy-Finch have gray on their hind-crown and on the side of their face (the amount varies geographically). The Black Rosy-Finch is considerably darker—even blackish—on its throat, breast, and mantle.

Habitat   Like all rosy-finches, Gray-crowneds are adapted to live in extreme environments. Although they breed at low elevations in the Aleutian and Pribilof islands, throughout most of their range they are found above timberline in mountains, usually near snow, and in rock piles and on cliffs. In the Aleutians and Pribilofs they are often found along beaches and in villages. In winter, montane populations move to lower elevations and are found in meadows, rocky hillsides, along roadsides, in towns, and even in cultivated areas; mixed flocks of rosy-finches often roost in abandoned mine shafts, which may be some distance from feeding sites, and individuals occasionally roost in abandoned woodpecker nests.

Behavior   Gray-crowned Rosy-Finches are found in barren, rocky areas, on cliffs near glaciers, and above timberline; in the Aleutian Islands, they are found among buildings in tundra. In winter, when they are generally found in flocks, often with other species of rosy-finches and sometimes with Horned Larks and American Pipits; they are found in open fields, brushy areas, around habitations, and at feeders. They are almost always seen on the ground, and unlike most finches they often walk when on the ground. In the breeding season, males are territorial, but generally defend only the area around the nest. Male-male aggression is common, and chases occur commonly during flight. They are also aggressive at feeders.

Voice   The song is a slow series of buzzy *chew* notes, *chew chew chew chew chew*, sometimes descending. The call is also *chew*.

Similar species   The Brown-capped Rosy-Finch lacks gray in the head, and females are a dark chocolate brown. Female Gray-crowned Rosy-Finches are like males in color but less brightly colored. Black Rosy-Finches are much darker than Gray-crowneds, and female Blacks show little pink.

Geographic variation   *L. t. griseonucha*, which breeds and winters in the Aleutian Islands (Near Islands), the Alaska Peninsula, and (occasionally) on Kodiak Island, Alaska, is very large (wing length 109–124 mm), and the back of the crown and ear coverts are uniformly gray; the throat is dusky, blending into the brown breast, and the body color is dark brown. *L. t. umbrina*, which is resident on the Pribilofs and St. Matthew Island in the Bering Sea, Alaska, is also large, with a blackish throat and very dark brown body color; likewise it has a gray cap and cheeks. *L. t. littoralis*, which breeds in west-central Alaska, southwestern Yukon, and northwestern British Columbia south to northern California, is like the above subspecies in color but lighter and smaller (wing length 96–110 mm). *L. t. tephrocotis*, which breeds in the mountains of northern Alaska south to southwestern Montana, is also smaller (wing length 97–111 mm) and is brown-cheeked. *L. t. wallowa*, which breeds in the Wallowa Mountains, Oregon, and winters south to central Nevada, is darker and less red brown than *L. t. littoralis*; it likewise has brown cheeks. *L. t. dawsoni* (resident in the Sierra Nevada and White Mountains of east-central California) is small and has brown cheeks, which contrast with the gray on the back of the crown. *L. t. wallowa* has a relatively large bill and has a dark brown back and nape (feathers often have distinctive dusky centers), and *L. t. dawsoni* has a relatively small, slender bill and dull brown upperparts.

Distribution   *Breeds* from w and n-central Alaska (north to the Seward Peninsula and the Brooks Range) and the Yukon (uncommon) south to s Alaska, and from Semidi Island, Kodiak Island, and the w Alaska Peninsula west through the eastern Aleutian Islands, Pribilof Islands, and St. Matthew (uncommon) and Nunivak islands, south to British Columbia (very rare on coast, fairly common in the s interior mountains) and sw Alberta, and in the mountains through the Cascades, Sierra Nevada, and Rocky Mountains to ne and central Oregon, e-central California, central Idaho, and nw Montana. Also found on the Commander Islands.

   Winters in the Aleutians, s mainland Alaska (rare), British Columbia (commonest in the southeast), s Alberta, and central Saskatchewan, south to w Oregon, central and e California, central Nevada, central Utah, n and central New Mexico, nw Nebraska, and sw South Dakota.

   Casual on St. Lawrence Island and in s Yukon east to s Manitoba, Minnesota, Iowa, Wisconsin, Illinois, Michigan, and Ohio, and south to s California. Accidental in central Yukon, w Ontario (Thunder Bay, Dryden), Quebec (St. Norbert), and Maine (Gorham).

Conservation status   Because of the extreme habitats in which they breed, little is known of changes in the numbers of Gray-crowned Rosy-Finches, but because of the remoteness of breeding sites, there is almost no direct impact from human activity on their breeding grounds. Global warming and glacial melt could be a threat, especially to the southern populations.

Molt   The First Basic plumage is acquired by a partial First Prebasic molt, the extent of which varies geographically; the body feathers are replaced, as are the median wing coverts and perhaps some of the inner greater coverts (in *L. t. griseonucha*), but none of the tertials or rectrices; the outer Juvenal median and greater wing coverts are retained. The Definitive Basic molt is complete and is initiated in mid-August and completed by late October (in the Sierra Nevada).

Description   Adult males—(*L. t. tephrocotis*) Forehead, forecrown, and lores black; sides of crown and hind-crown silver gray; sides of head brown; nape, sides of neck, ***back***, and scapulars cinnamon brown; back and scapular feather have buff margins and black feather shafts; uppertail coverts and ***rump*** brown with broad pink tips; ***tail*** gray; throat and chin dark; otherwise ***underparts*** pinkish brown, with pale undertail coverts, flecked with dark brown. **Adult females**—Similar to males but black in the crown duller, and pink in body areas duller. There appears to be no Prealternate molt, but color changes occur due to feather wear. **First-winter birds** are like Basic-plumage birds but less brightly colored. ***Bill*** charcoal gray to black during the breeding season, yellowish during fall and winter; males retain the black bill color longer than females; ***legs*** and ***feet*** black; ***iris*** brown.

Hybrids   There are hybrids with the Black Rosy-Finch in the Bitterroot Mountains in Idaho and Montana, Seven Devils Mountains, Idaho, and Little Belt Mountains, Montana.

References   Clement et al. (1993), MacDougall-Shackleton et al. (2000), Pyle (1997), Winker et al. (2003).

25.1 Definitive male Gray-crowned Rosy-Finch *Leucosticte t. umbrina*, St. Paul Island, Pribilof Islands, Alaska, USA, July 2004. All rosy-finches are medium-sized finches with short legs and very long primary extension. This form is considerably larger than the mainland forms. Mostly rich chocolate brown spangled with pink on belly, with contrasting black crown and throat and pale gray face and nape. Wings with much pink edging to coverts and flight feathers. Bill black in summer (Larry Sansone).

25.2 Female Gray-crowned Rosy-Finch *Leucosticte t. umbrina*, St. Paul Island, Pribilof Islands, Alaska, USA, 2004. Duller than male, with less distinct head pattern and considerably less pink in wing. Underparts mostly brown, with very little pink spangling on flanks (Larry Sansone).

25.3 Adult Gray-crowned Rosy-Finch *Leucosticte t. littoralis*, Homer, Alaska, USA, March 2000. Similar to Bering Sea birds but smaller, and with paler chocolate brown mantle and underparts. Note extensive rosy pink spangling on lower back and rump. Wings show extensive pink on greater coverts and edges to flight feathers (Brian E. Small).

25.4 Immature Gray-crowned Rosy-Finch *Leucosticte t. littoralis*, Sandia Crest, New Mexico, USA, December 2001. Duller than breeding adult, with grayish brown mantle and underparts and limited rosy pink spangling on rear flanks. Blackish crown patch rather diffuse. Wings lack pink edges on greater coverts and flight feathers. All rosy-finches have yellow bills in winter (Phil Kelly).

25.5 Basic adult Gray-crowned Rosy-Finch *Leucosticte t. littoralis*, Tonopah, Nevada, USA, December 2000. Similar to breeding adult but bill yellow, with dark tip. In fresh plumage, as here, body feathers are narrowly edged in gray, creating a scaly appearance. Generally brighter than the immature, with some pink on greater coverts and flight feathers (Herbert Clarke).

25.6 Spring male Gray-crowned Rosy-Finch *Leucosticte t. tephrocotis*, Inyo County, California, USA, April 1993. Differs from other forms by lacking gray cheeks. Body mostly warm chocolate brown, whiter on undertail coverts, with extensive rosy pink spangling on belly and flanks. Greater coverts and flight feathers edged pink. Note black bill on this spring bird (Larry Sansone).

25.7 Female Gray-crowned Rosy-Finch *Leucosticte t. tephrocotis*, Ellery Lake, California, USA, July 1989. Similar to Alternate male but duller overall, with less well-defined head pattern. Shows far less rosy pink on underparts, but note that this midsummer bird is in very worn plumage. Slight pink tinge to greater coverts (Mike Danzenbaker).

25.8 Basic adult Gray-crowned Rosy-Finch *Leucosticte t. tephrocotis,* Tonopah, Nevada, USA, December 2000. Like Spring male, but with bill mostly yellow and body plumage scaled buffy gray. Note the very long primary extension common to all rosy-finches. In mixed winter flocks, best distinguished from similarly patterned Black Rosy-Finch by brown body plumage and brown cheeks (Herbert Clarke).

25.9 Immature Gray-crowned Rosy-Finch *Leucosticte t. tephrocotis,* Tonopah, Nevada, USA, December 2000. Similar to Basic adult but duller, with less well-defined head pattern and little rosy pink spangling on underparts. Wings show whitish edges to greater coverts and flight feathers. In mixed winter flocks, look for relatively well-defined gray hind-crown and brown body plumage (Herbert Clarke).

26 Black Rosy-Finch

(*Leucosticte atrata*)

Measurements

Length: 14.0–17.0 cm; 5.5–6.7 in.

Wing: 96–111 mm; 3.8–4.4 in. (males somewhat larger than females).

Mass: Males (summer) 21.9–31.5 g, av. 25.1 g; females (summer) 20.7–32.0 g, av. 25.4 g. Males (winter) 22.9–31.5 g, av. 26.9 g; females (winter) 22.0–28.3 g, av. 24.2 g.

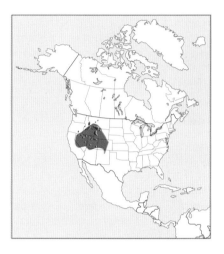

The Black Rosy-Finch breeds in scattered mountain ranges of the western United States and is found between the ranges of the northern Gray-crowned Rosy-Finch and the Brown-capped Rosy-Finch of the central and southern Rocky Mountains. It is the darkest of the rosy-finches and is generally easily distinguished in the field.

Habitat Black Rosy-Finches breed in alpine tundra and meadows, often in barren, rocky areas or grassy areas. In winter they move to lower elevations and occur in fields, brushy areas, and often around human habitations (they come to feeders). In winter they sometimes roost in caves, under bridges, in mine shafts, or in open buildings.

Behavior Like other rosy-finches, males are territorial but defend a floating territory around their mate during the breeding season, accompanying her everywhere during the early breeding season. In winter, they are gregarious and usually are found in flocks that include other species of rosy-finches. They often share winter roosts with other rosy-finches and sometimes other species (e.g., starlings and House Sparrows). They readily come to feeders. They walk as well as hop on the ground.

Voice The voice of the Black Rosy-Finch is like that of the Gray-crowned Rosy-Finch, and the song is given by males only.

Similar species See the account of the Gray-crowned Rosy-Finch.

Geographic variation No geographic variation has been described.

Distribution *Breeds* in the mountains from s-central Oregon (Steens Mountain and perhaps Wallowa Mountains), central Idaho, sw and s-central Montana and n-central Wyoming south to ne and e-central Nevada (south to the Snake Mountains) and central Utah (Tushar and La Sal mountains).

Winters from central Idaho and se Wyoming south to s Nevada, n Arizona, and n and central New Mexico.

Casual in winter to e Oregon, e California, and e Montana. Accidental in Ohio (Conneaut).

Conservation status   Because of the remoteness of their breeding habitat, it is unlikely that the numbers of Black Rosy-Finches are adversely affected by human activities. They are more vulnerable in winter, when they are concentrated at roosts, feeders, or along roads.

Molt   Little is known about the Prejuvenal molt, which takes place before the young fledge. The First Basic plumage is acquired by a partial First Prebasic molt during which body feathers, most of the median and lesser coverts, and perhaps a few of the greater wing coverts are replaced. The Definitive Basic plumage is acquired by a complete Definitive Prebasic molt, which occurs mostly in August.

Description   Adult males—*Head* blackish, except for black on the hind-crown, which is gray; mantle and scapulars blackish or dark brown; *rump* and uppertail coverts rose, with dark brown centers to feathers; rectrices dark brown, with rosy edges; throat and upper breast black to dark brown; flanks rosy, with dark brown streaks; belly dark brown, edged with rose or whitish, or rosy; undertail coverts pink, with brown centers to feathers; median and greater coverts dark brown, broadly edged with rose. **Adult females**—Similar to males but with lighter colors; when pink appears on the *underparts* it is confined to the belly. There is no Prealternate molt in this species, but wear changes the individual's appearance in the breeding season, generally making them appear darker in coloration. **First-year individuals**—Similar to Definitive Basic plumage in both sexes, but some Juvenal coverts are retained and are worn and brownish. *Bill* yellow but often with a black tip in winter, and black during the breeding season; *legs* and *feet* black; *iris* dark brown.

Hybrids   Black Rosy-Finches have hybridized with Gray-crowned Rosy-Finches where their ranges overlap.

References   Johnson (2002), Udvardy (1977).

26.1 Adult Black Rosy-Finch *Leucosticte atrata*, Hailey, Idaho, USA, March 1997. Shares a similar head pattern with interior form of Gray-crowned Rosy-Finch, differing mostly by blackish face, mantle, and upper underparts. Shows extensive pink edges to greater coverts and flight feathers but relatively little rosy spangling on belly and flanks. Note that the bill is still mostly yellow on this early spring bird (Brian E. Small).

26.2 Basic male Black Rosy-Finch *Leucosticte atrata*, Tonopah, Nevada, USA, December 2000. Similar to spring male but body plumage heavily fringed with grayish buff, creating a scaly appearance. Head pattern sharply defined. Wings show much pink on coverts and flight feathers. Bill mostly yellow, with dark tip (Larry Sansone).

26.3 Basic male Black Rosy-Finch *Leucosticte atrata*, Tonopah, Nevada, USA, December 2000. Another view of a male showing the overall blackness of the face and body. Again, rather a lot of pink in the wing but relatively little on the underparts. Note how sharply demarcated the gray hind-crown is from the blackish forecrown and auriculars (Herbert Clarke).

26.4 Immature male Black Rosy-Finch *Leucosticte atrata*, Sandia Crest, New Mexico, USA, December 2001. Considerably duller and grayer than mature male, with reduced pink on wings and underparts. Similar to immature female Brown-capped Rosy-Finch but colder looking, with darker gray cheeks and throat and more sharply defined gray hind-crown (Phil Kelly).

26.5 Winter flock of Black and Brown-capped rosy-finches *Leucosticte atrata* and *Leucosticte australis,* Sandia Crest, New Mexico, USA, December 2001. Note the black-and-gray appearance of the Black Rosy-Finches compared with the warmer brown tones of the two Brown-capped (*center and foreground right*). Note also the very scaly appearance of the female Black (*third from left*) compared with the two males to her left (Phil Kelly).

27 Brown-capped Rosy-Finch

(Leucosticte australis)

Measurements
Length: 15.0–17.0 cm; 5.9–6.7 in.
Wing: 97–112 mm; 3.8–4.4 in. (males somewhat larger than females).
Mass: Male av. 26.9 g (n = 35, early July); female av. 27.8 g (n = 13, early July).

Generally, Brown-capped Rosy-Finches are the only rosy-finches with no gray on their head, although some individuals have a rather diffuse gray supercilium. They are found only in the southern Rocky Mountains, from southeastern Wyoming south to north-central New Mexico.

Habitat Like other species in this genus, Brown-capped Rosy-Finches breed in alpine habitats and in montane cliffs and grassy areas. They winter at lower elevations in open fields, brushy areas, and around human habitations. They often roost in old Cliff Swallow nests, caves, and barns.

Behavior In summer, this species is most frequently seen feeding on insects frozen on the surface of snow and on seeds exposed as the snowfields melt. These birds migrate in flocks during the daytime and flock in winter, often with other rosy-finches. On the ground they walk or (less often) hop, looking for seeds, and allow humans close approach.

Voice The song is similar to that of other rosy-finches; they have a *chirp* alarm note that is similar to the chirp of House Sparrows. Their flight call is a faint *peent*.

Similar species See the account of the Gray-crowned Rosy-Finch.

Geographic variation No subspecies have been described.

Distribution *Breeds* in the mountains of se Wyoming (Medicine Bow Range) south through Colorado to n New Mexico (Santa Fe region).

Winters at lower elevations in the breeding range. There are no records for adjacent states (Utah, Arizona, Kansas, or Nebraska), and the one record from n-central Oklahoma is best considered hypothetical.

Conservation status Because Brown-capped Rosy-Finches are found only in remote alpine habitats, it is unlikely that human activities have affected their numbers, although they are sometimes killed as they forage along roadsides in winter.

Molt   The First Basic plumage is obtained by a partial First Prebasic molt, during which the body feathers, and some or most of the lesser and median and the three innermost greater wing coverts, are lost. There is no Prealternate molt. The Definitive Basic plumage is acquired by a complete Definitive Prebasic molt; molting occurs in late August into early October.

Description   Adult males—There is a dark cap that is paler posteriorly and with a variable, diffuse broad gray supercilium; sides of the face, nape, and mantle brown, with faint brown streaks on the mantle; uppertail coverts brown, boldly edged with white or light rose; *tail* brown; *underparts* brown, becoming faintly washed with rose, flecked with brown on the belly; undertail coverts whitish, edged with brown; lesser, middle, and greater wing coverts edged with pink or rose; remiges dusky brown. **Adult females**—Similar to adult males but much grayer and paler. Their brown cap varies from being distinct to indistinct. **First-winter individuals** resemble adult females but are less pink, and they retain some worn Juvenal coverts, remiges, and rectrices. *Bill* of males in breeding season is black, and lemon yellow in winter; females are similar but colors less intense than males; young birds have yellowish bills; *legs* and *feet* black; *iris* dark brown.

Hybrids   No hybrids have been described.

References   Johnson (1977), Johnson et al. (2000), Pyle (1997), Sibley (2000), Udvardy (1977).

27.1 Definitive Alternate male Brown-capped Rosy-Finch *Leucosticte australis*, Rocky Mountain National Park, Colorado, USA, July 1992. Mostly warm chocolate brown mantle and head, with darker central crown unique among rosy-finches. Note also more extensive rosy pink spangling on belly and flanks and bright pink edges to wing coverts and flight feathers. Bill black (Herbert Clarke).

27.2 Definitive Alternate male Brown-capped Rosy-Finch *Leucosticte australis*, Mount Evans, Colorado, USA, June 2001. This front view clearly shows the extensively brown head, slightly grayer above the eye and contrasting with the blackish crown. Note also the large rosy pink patch on the belly and flanks (Kevin T. Karlson).

27.3 Female Brown-capped Rosy-Finch *Leucosticte australis*, Rocky Mountain National Park, Colorado, USA, July 1992. Similar to breeding male, but with considerably less rosy pink on belly and flanks. Body plumage is slightly grayer overall, due to pale fringes to feathers, and the head shows some gray around bill and on supercilium (Herbert Clarke).

27.4 Basic-plumaged Brown-capped and Black rosy-finches *Leucosticte australis* and *Leucosticte atrata*, Sandia Crest, New Mexico, USA, December 2001. Overall rather grayish brown, with body feathers fringed gray, creating scaly appearance. *From front left*: Immature Brown-capped, adult male Black (mostly hidden), immature Black, and male Brown-capped at rear right. Immature Brown-capped and Black rather similar but no black feather centers on mantle of Black (Phil Kelly).

2 8 Pine Grosbeak

(Pinicola enucleator)

Measurements
Length: 20.0–25.5 cm; 7.9–10.0 in.
Wing: 101–125 mm; 4.0–5.0 in. (males slightly larger than females).
Mass: 52.0–62.0 g (Canada); avs. 60.3 g (Canada taiga), 58.0 g (Alaska taiga), 57.0 g (Alaska coast), 54.6 g (Rocky Mtns.), 47.4 g (Sierra Nevada).

Pine Grosbeaks are large, colorful finches of the boreal forests of both North America and Eurasia. One population of Pine Grosbeaks breeds in the taiga of northern and central Canada and Alaska, whereas others are found in the montane West. In winter, the northern birds are to a certain extent irruptive and gregarious, but only uncommonly do they move south of southern Canada and the northernmost states. The montane birds move little seasonally and rarely wander far from their breeding sites.

Habitat   Pine Grosbeaks breed in open coniferous woodlands, mostly spruce and fir, or in some areas in lodgepole pine or mixed forest, characteristically near water. In Alaska, beyond the tree line, they are found in alder thickets. In migration and winter, they can occur in a variety of woodlands and second growth. They may be found in habitats determined to some extent by the availability of foods such as mountain ash, ash, maple, and holly (*Ilex* sp.).

Behavior   Pine Grosbeaks are more often heard than seen as they utter their distinctive flight calls. Males often sing from the tops or near the tops of coniferous trees. They mostly feed on buds, seeds, or fruits, which they pick from trees or from the ground. In spring, they especially feed on the fresh growth of conifers, and can cause damage to pine plantations. On the ground, they either walk or hop, and their flight is slightly undulating. They occasionally flycatch rather clumsily. During the breeding season, males sing from the tops or near the tops of coniferous trees. In migration and winter they are gregarious but usually do not flock with other finches. In the northern parts of their range (northern Canada, Alaska) they readily come to feeders, but uncommonly do so in southern Ontario. During all seasons they are easily approached.

Voice   The flight calls of Pine Grosbeaks are geographically variable. In winter, in areas where two or more call types occur, birds tend to flock with others with the same call type. The flight call of taiga birds is a loud, raspy *tee-tee-tew* and reminiscent of

Greater Yellowlegs, whereas that of birds from the Rockies is a fruity *blurp-blurp*; the call of the Sierra birds is a bit like that of the Rocky Mountain birds. Their song is a lazy, clear series of modulated or unmodulated whistles that often mimic the songs of other species. It is said to resemble the song of the Purple Finch, with the tonal qualities of eastern Fox Sparrows.

Similar species The large size of the Pine Grosbeak, as well as its coloration, make this species easy to distinguish from other finches. The white wing bars and the coloration of the males are like that of the smaller White-winged Crossbill, but these two are easily distinguished.

Geographic variation Six subspecies have been described from North America. Two are widespread. *P. e. leucurus* breeds from central Alaska east through the taiga forest to Quebec, Newfoundland, and the Maritime Provinces. Some recognize separate subspecies in Alaska (*P. e. alascensis*) and in Newfoundland, the Maritimes, and southern Quebec (*P. e. eschatosus*), but geographic variation in the taiga is broadly clinal. *P. e. leucurus* are variable in size and have back feathers with indistinct (females) or distinct (males) dusky centers; the flanks of males are medium pinkish red to red, with little or no grayish mottling. *P. e. montanus* breeds from central British Columbia south in the mountains to Arizona and New Mexico. It is large, and its back feathers lack or have indistinct dusky centers; the breast of males is medium dark red with gray mottling, and the males are oranger and the females yellower in hue than *P. e. leucurus*. *P. e. flammula* of coastal Alaska and northern British Columbia is medium in size and large billed, and males have little if any gray mottling in their breast plumage (i.e., their plumage resembles that of *P. e. montanus*, but the red on the belly and flanks of the males is more extensive). *P. e. carlottae* is resident in the Queen Charlotte Islands, British Columbia. It is small, with a medium-sized bill. Otherwise, it resembles *P. e. flammula*. *P. e. californicus*, which is resident in montane eastern California, is of medium size with a small bill; it resembles *P. e. flammula* or *P. e. montana*. *P. e. kamtschatkensis*, which is casual in the Aleutians and on the Pribilof Islands, is smaller than *P. e. flammula*, with a narrow, strongly hooked bill.

Distribution Circumpolar. In North America **breeds** from w and central Alaska, s Yukon, sw and central Mackenzie, n Manitoba (fairly common), n Ontario, n Quebec and Labrador (north to the tree line), and Newfoundland south to southern Alaska (west to the base of the Alaska Peninsula and Kodiak Island), British Columbia (Queen Charlotte Islands, s interior mountains), w Alberta, central and ne Oregon (Wheeler, Grant, Union, and Wallowa counties; uncommon), central California (southern Sierra Nevada), extreme w-central Nevada, n and e-central Arizona, n New Mexico, and, east of the Rockies, to n Alberta, n Saskatchewan, central and se Manitoba, s-central Ontario, n Michigan (rare), sw Quebec, n New Hampshire, n Vermont, central Maine, and Nova Scotia.

   Winters in North America from w and central Alaska, central (rare) and s Yukon, s Mackenzie, and s Canada south through the breeding range, and sporadically as far as central New Mexico, se Colorado, n and n-central Texas, nw Oklahoma, w and central Kansas, n-central Arkansas, Missouri, Kentucky, Virginia, and the Carolinas.

Conservation status Because this species both breeds and winters in places where there are few people, it status is not well known. In northern Europe, Pine Grosbeaks have declined in places such as northern Finland, where there has been extensive cutting of forests, and that is probably also true in North America. They are attracted to salt that has been spread along roads, where many are killed.

Molt   The First Basic plumage is acquired by a partial Prebasic molt that takes place from July through late September. The Definitive Basic plumage is acquired by a complete Prebasic molt from late July to late September (usually in early August).

Description   Adult males—*Head, back,* throat, breast, belly, and flanks (variable) and *rump* deep brick red to slightly orangish red; lower breast, undertail coverts, and (sometimes) throat and flanks gray; *wings* black with two white wing bars and white edges to secondaries and tertials; *tail* blackish. **First-year males**—Similar to adult females. **Adult females**—Similar to males, but with a light greenish *head* and *rump* (some individuals are russet) and a gray *back* and undersides. **Juveniles**—Like females but brownish gray on the *head* and undersides. *Bill* black or dark gray; *legs* and *feet* brown to black; *iris* dark brown.

Hybrids   The Pine Grosbeak has been reported to hybridize with the Purple Finch. In captivity they have hybridized with either *Loxia* or *Carduelis*. Hybridization with European Bullfinches in captivity has not produced viable offspring.

References   Adkisson (1977, 1999), Clement et al. (1993), Pyle (1997).

28.1 Male Pine Grosbeak *Pinicola e. leucurus*, Algonquin Provincial Park, Ontario, Canada, March 2004. A large, long-tailed finch with small head and rather stubby bill. Head and body mostly pinkish red, with gray scapulars and flanks. Black wings show broad white tips to median and greater coverts. Note short black eye line, contrasting with pale gray crescent below eye. Bill blackish (Sam Barone).

28.2 Male Pine Grosbeak *Pinicola e. leucurus*, Churchill, Manitoba, Canada, June 1988. In this back view note the white wing bars and white edges to tertials. Longish black tail has a noticeable notch at tip. The rather short, blackish bill has a curved culmen and a short hook at tip (Greg W. Lasley).

28.3 Female Pine Grosbeak *Pinicola e. leucurus*, Sibley Provincial Park, Ontario, Canada, October 1991. Females from all populations are rather similar in appearance. Mostly gray with bronzy yellow wash on crown, auriculars, and rump. Wings with bold white tips to greater coverts and white edges to tertials. Note rather small, rounded head, stubby bill, and deeply notched tail (David D. Beadle).

28.4 Pine Grosbeak *Pinicola e. leucurus*, Algonquin Provincial Park, Ontario, Canada, March 2004. Immature males and some females show reddish orange or russet coloration on crown, ear coverts, and rump. Otherwise the plumage is mostly midgray like adult female's. The amount of reddish feathering on the breast of this individual perhaps indicates it is a second-calendar-year male (Sam Barone).

28.5 Male Pine Grosbeak *Pinicola e. montanus*, Glacier National Park, Montana, USA, June 1997. Although highly variable, males from the Rocky Mountains tend to show more gray in body plumage than *Pinicola e. leucurus*. This bird shows extensive gray on more uniform, unspotted mantle and along flanks. Some individuals can be even grayer on underparts (Brian E. Small).

28.6 Female Pine Grosbeak *Pinicola e. montanus*, Glacier National Park, Montana, USA, June 1997. Gray overall with variable tones of yellow olive on crown, auriculars, and rump (not visible here). White wing bars and tertial edging are evident. Large size, distinctive structure, and essentially gray plumage separate this species from other finches (Brian E. Small).

28.7 Male Pine Grosbeak *Pinicola e. alascensis*, Seward, Alaska, USA, July 1999. Similar to other Pine Grosbeaks and likewise somewhat variable, but males tend to average deeper red head and body plumage. Note especially extensively reddish mantle. Gray flanks contrast with whitish undertail coverts and bright red rump (Rick and Nora Bowers).

29 Common Rosefinch

(Carpodacus erythrinus)

Measurements
Length: 14.5–15.0 cm; 5.7–5.9 in.
Wing: 78–90 mm; 3.1–3.5 in. (sexes similar in size).
Mass: 21.0–30.0 g, av. 24.1 g.

The Common Rosefinch is extralimital in our area. There have been about two dozen records since 1972, all but one from Alaska.

Habitat   Common Rosefinches are found in wet woodlands, forest edges, riparian thickets (willows or tamarisk), thickets in taiga, and around human habitations.

Behavior   In their usual range they are fairly gregarious in the nonbreeding season and sometimes associate with other fringillids.

Voice   The song of the Common Rosefinch is described as a monotonous, repeated whistling *weeeja-wu-weeeja*; it rarely sings outside of the breeding season. The call is a rising whistled *ooeet* or *too-ee*.

Similar species   Compare this bird with other *Carpodacus*, none of which normally occur in the geographic area where Common Rosefinches appear. The bill shape of the rosefinch is more like that of the House Finch than that of other American *Carpodacus*, but the breast and belly of rosefinches are unstreaked or (females) only lightly streaked. The red on male rosefinches (of the subspecies that appears in the Americas) is virtually confined to the head, breast, and rump.

Geographic variation   *C. e. grebnitskii* of eastern Siberia is the subspecies that migrates irregularly through western Alaska.

Distribution   *Breeds* from s Finland, n Russia, and n Siberia south to central Europe, Asia Minor, the Himalayas, Mongolia, and n China.
   Winters principally from India east through Southeast Asia and s China.
   Migrates irregularly in spring through the w Aleutians (Attu, Buldir) and St. Lawrence Island, and occasionally to the Pribilofs (St. Paul). First North American record was from the Yukon-Kuskokwim Delta, Alaska (Old Kashunuk Village), but all others have been from the w Aleutians, Pribilofs, and St. Lawrence Island. Casual in the fall in the w Aleutians (Shemya, 31 August), and in fall to St. Lawrence Island (Gambell).

Conservation status   The Common Rosefinch is extralimital in our area but is locally common in its Eurasian range.

Molt   There is a complete Prebasic molt, September to November.

Description   Adult males—*Head*, throat, and upper breast rose red; *rump* reddish; *wings* and *tail* brown; belly and flanks pale beige, thinly streaked with red. **Adult females**—Like adult males but grayish brown above, with no red; breast thinly streaked with brown. *Legs* and *feet* brown or pinkish brown; *bill* grayish or dark grayish brown.

Hybrids   In captivity, Common Rosefinches have been hybridized with Purple Finches, and hybrids with Greenfinches *(Carduelis carduelis)* have been reported.

References   Clement et al. (1993), Cramp and Perrins (1994a), Dau and Gibson (1974), Dunn et al. (2002), Kessel and Gibson (1978).

29.1 Male Common Rosefinch *Carpodacus e. erythrinus*, North Yorkshire, UK, August 2004. A medium-size *Carpodacus* finch with a rather stubby, rounded bill and long primary extension. Head and breast mostly pinkish red. Upperparts grayish brown, with pinkish red rump and pink-tinged wing bars. Underparts mostly uniform whitish. Males of the form *C. e. grebnitskii*, the form most likely to occur in Alaska, are slightly darker overall, with redder head and breast and more extensive reddish tones on mantle (George Reszeter).

29.2 Female or First Summer male Common Rosefinch *Carpodacus e. grebnitskii*, Gambell, St. Lawrence Island, Alaska, USA, September 2003. Duller than male, lacking red head and breast. Mostly pale grayish brown with fine, dusky streaking on crown, neck, and breast. Could be confused with a female House Finch but note more restricted streaking on underparts (Phil Davis).

29.3 Juvenile or First Basic Common Rosefinch *Carpodacus e. erythrinus*, Isles of Scilly, UK, October 1994. Overall pale grayish brown, with fine, dusky streaking on crown, mantle, and breast. Wings dusky brown, with pale buff tips and edges to coverts and tertials. Underparts mostly whitish, with some dark streaking along flanks. Beady eye stands out on plain face. Compared with female House Finch, note paler overall appearance, whiter, less streaky underparts, and longer primary extension (George Reszeter).

3 0 Purple Finch

(Carpodacus purpureus)

Measurements
Length: 13.5–16.0 cm; 5.3–6.3 in.
Wing: 71–87 mm; 2.8–3.4 in. (males somewhat larger than females).
Mass: 18.1–35.3 g, av. 24.9 g (Pennsylvania).

The male Purple Finch, with its raspberry coloration and complex rambling warbling song, is a fairly conspicuous bird during the breeding season; females and young birds are chunky, drab sparrow-like birds.

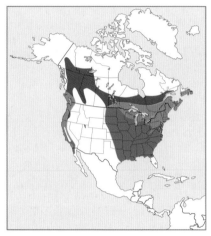

Habitat Purple Finches breed in coastal rain forests (in the West), in moist open mixed and coniferous (especially spruce and fir) forests and second growth, and in parks and orchards. In California they occur in riparian oak or oak-conifer woodlands. In migration and winter, they are found in a variety of woodland and woodland edge areas, and around human habitations. In the East they commonly come to feeders.

Behavior Males apparently defend territories, and often sing from near the nests. In winter, Purple Finches are often found in small flocks, and during aggressive interactions female-plumaged birds displace males more frequently than would be expected by chance. They may sally from a perch to catch insects, and their flight is undulating. On the ground, they usually hop but will walk short distances.

Voice Three song types have been described. The warbling song is six to twenty-three rapid, connected elements with no two consecutive elements on the same pitch. The territory song is a series of rapid notes on the same pitch. The "vireo" song consists of phrases of two to five notes that is reminiscent of warbling vireo song. The flight call is a sharp *tick* or *bik*; the quality of this call is different in the East and West. Western birds give a *cheer-lee* call.

Similar species Purple Finches are most easily confused with other *Carpodacus*. The red on male House Finches is usually brighter and oranger, not raspberry colored as on the Purple Finch, and the red on House Finches is confined to the crown, throat, and chest, whereas on the Purple Finch the red is also on the head, back, and flanks, often extending farther down on the belly than it does on the House Finch. The bill of the House Finch is short and curved, whereas that of Purple Finch is stout with a slightly curved culmen. The ventral streaking on female House Finches is blurry, whereas the dark ventral streaks on female Purple Finches (especially eastern birds) are distinct.

Eastern female-plumage Purple Finches have a broad, pale supercilium and a pale, diffuse submoustachial stripe outlining the dark brown ear coverts (these stripes are much less distinct on western birds); House Finches have a brown head. Cassin's Finches have a sharp, conical bill with a straight culmen. Male Cassin's Finches are rosy pink, have a bright red crown that contrasts with the rest of the head, and have a brown-streaked nape; their flanks are whitish, although they may be lightly washed with red. Cassin's Finches often appear to be slightly crested (as do some Purple Finches), and they have a longer primary projection than even eastern Purple Finches. Female Cassin's Finches have a facial pattern like that of eastern female-plumaged Purple Finches, but with brown streaks in the buffy supercilium and submoustachial stripes (sometimes obscuring them) and with sparse, crisp ventral streaking. In flight their underwing coverts are gray, whereas those of Purple Finches are pallid. Pine Grosbeaks are larger, have a different-shaped bill, a different body shape, and two distinct wing bars.

Geographic variation   Two subspecies are generally recognized; their ranges are nearly disjunct (they are found coast to coast in the boreal forest of central Canada), and they are fairly well defined. Adult male western *C. p. californicus* have a dull pinkish rose head that is paler than the rump, whereas male eastern *C. p. purpureus* have a bright reddish head that contrasts with the pale pinkish rump, which is often slightly purplish. The undertail coverts of female and hatching-year male *C. p. californicus* have blackish streaking (which may be indistinct), whereas those of *C. p. purpureus* lack or have indistinct streaking. Female-plumaged *C. p. purpureus* have a broad, somewhat diffuse pale supercilium and a submoustachial stripe that outline dark brown ear coverts, whereas female-plumaged *C. p. californicus* have an indistinct facial pattern. Female-plumaged *C. p. californicus* appear to be a richer chocolate brown with blurry ventral streaks, whereas female-plumaged *C. p. purpureus* are darker brown with fairly distinct ventral streaks. *C. p. purpureus* average larger than *C. p. californicus* and have longer primary projection. *C. p. purpureus* are recorded casually in California.

Distribution   *Breeds* from central and ne British Columbia, s Yukon, sw Mackenzie, n and central Alberta, central Saskatchewan, central Manitoba, n Ontario, s Quebec (north to 50°N, including Anticosti Island), and s Newfoundland south (w of the Cascades and in the Sierra Nevada) to s California, central and ne Oregon (rare), and (east of the Great Plains) to central Alberta, se Saskatchewan, n-central North Dakota, nw and central Minnesota, central Wisconsin, central Michigan, n Ohio, West Virginia, central Pennsylvania, and se New York.

   Winters from sw British Columbia south through w Washington, central and w Oregon, and California to Baja California and rarely east across central and s Arizona to s New Mexico (rare), and in the east from s Manitoba (rare), s Ontario, s Quebec (to 48°N), New Brunswick, Prince Edward Island, Nova Scotia, and s Newfoundland south to central and se Texas, the Gulf Coast, and central and s Florida (casual).

   Casual elsewhere in w North America from e-central, s-coastal, and se Alaska, e Washington, Idaho, and w Montana south to n Arizona, New Mexico, and extreme w Texas, and north to Nunavut (off Resolution Island) and Labrador (Cartwright). Accidental on St. Lawrence Island in the Bering Sea.

Conservation status   Although nowhere a particularly common bird, Purple Finches are not threatened. Moderate logging may benefit them, as they like fairly open forests. In some areas feeders probably provide an important source of food in winter.

Molt The First Prebasic plumage is acquired by a partial First Prebasic molt in which the Juvenal remiges and rectrices are not replaced; this occurs August to October. There apparently is no First Prealternate molt. The Definitive Basic molt is complete and occurs July to November, and there is a partial Definitive Alternate molt, at least in some males, in which some feathers in the front of the head are replaced; this occurs in April.

Description Adult males—Crown and superciliaum purplish red (occasionally a brighter red); ear coverts brownish, washed in red; *back* and wing coverts mottled brownish, washed in red; *rump* solid red, lighter in color than the crown; *underparts* purplish red, with a white belly and undertail coverts, although undertail coverts may be washed in buffy pink; blurry, obscure streaks on the flanks. **Adult females**—Crown and *back* chocolate brown and heavily mottled; supercilium and submoustachial stripe pale buffy; a buffy crescent under the eye and a few thin brown streaks (these buffy areas are obscure in western birds); *back* brownish with distinct brown streaks; *rump* lighter than back, with dark brown centers; remiges and rectrices brown; throat buffy with thin brown speckles; malar dark brown (in eastern birds) or brown (western birds); *underparts* pale with dark brown streaks on the breast and flanks; undertail coverts whitish with a few brown flecks; western birds are a paler chocolate brown, and the ventral streaks are blurry. **First-year birds** of both sexes resemble adult females. *Bill* dark brown, darkest at the tip; *legs* and *feet* dark brown; *iris* dark brown.

Hybrids Hybrids with the Pine Grosbeak and perhaps with the House Finch have been reported.

References Clement et al. (1993), Kaufman (1990), Pyle (1997), Wootton (1996).

30.1 Male Purple Finch *Carpodacus p. purpureus*, Central Park, New York City, New York, USA, October 1998. A chunky *Carpodacus* finch with shortish tail, large head, and stout, slightly curved bill. Reddish overall, with pinkish highlights on head and underparts. Belly and undertail coverts uniform white, with some blurry streaking on rear flanks. Male House Finch is longer tailed and has bold, dusky streaking along flanks (Michael D. Stubblefield).

30.2 Female or First Basic male Purple Finch *Carpodacus p. purpureus*, Central Park, New York City, New York, USA, October 2001. Upperparts mostly brown. Striking head pattern, with whitish supercilium behind eye and streaky white malar and arc below eye. Underparts white, buffy on flanks, and thickly spotted with brown on sides of throat, breast, and along flanks. Differs from House Finch by overall structure, more contrasting head pattern, and bill shape (Michael D. Stubblefield).

30.3 Male Purple Finch *Carpodacus p. californicus*, Mount Pinos, California, USA, July 1997. West Coast birds are similar to birds from the East but tend to have slightly more curved culmen, making the bill appear more rounded, and show somewhat more brownish streaking along flanks. Otherwise, note reddish head and breast, with pinkish highlights (Brian E. Small).

30.4 Female or First Summer male Purple Finch *Carpodacus p. californicus*, Mount Pinos, California, USA, July 1994. Similar to eastern female or First summer male but drabber, with olive-tinged upperparts and less distinct, blurry streaking on whitish underparts. Head pattern is less sharply defined, with much streaking on pale supercilium and malar area (Brian E. Small).

30.5 Juvenal Purple Finch *Carpodacus p. californicus*, Mount Pinos, California, USA, July 1994. Similar to female but very drab and more uniformly olive brown. Even though the head pattern is indistinct, there are traces of the pale supercilium and crescent below eye. Note extensive, blurry brown streaking on breast and flanks. Yellow gape obvious (Brian E. Small).

3 1 Cassin's Finch

(Carpodacus cassinii)

Measurements
Length: 14.5–15.5 cm; 5.7–6.1 in.
Wing: 84–98 mm; 3.3–3.9 in. (males larger than females).
Mass: 20.4–37.8 g, av. 26.5 g (Arizona).

In the coniferous forests of the interior mountains of western North America, Cassin's Finch is one of the commonest and most conspicuous songbirds. It is most similar to the more widespread, closely related Purple Finch but, at least in summer, is usually found at higher elevations. In the mountains of southern California, there is much altitudinal overlap between the two species. The Cassin's Finch has a long conical bill, and its culmen is straighter than that of the Purple Finch. Males are rose red, whereas male Purple Finches are more raspberry red, and Cassin's Finches often appear to be slightly crested.

Habitat   Cassin's Finches breed in montane open coniferous forests, often at high elevation. They often are found in mature lodgepole or ponderosa pine forests but are also found in other pines, Douglas fir, spruce, or fir forests. They occasionally breed in open sagebrush shrubsteppe with scattered junipers. In migration and winter they move to lower elevations or southward, and in migration and winter are also found in brushy areas. They are usually found in pairs or small flocks, often with other fringillids, and may visit feeders.

Behavior   Males establish a territory when females begin to seek a nesting site. At this time, males reduce their singing and evict other males either by threat displays or by chases. They often forage away from the territory. Cassin's Finches tend to feed on buds, seeds, or berries, either at the top of trees or on the ground, and often erect their crown feathers. Their flight is undulating, and they hop when on the ground.

Voice   Their song is variable. It is a long, bright warble, higher than that of western Purple Finches, and they frequently mimic other songbirds (e.g., Red Crossbills), incorporating elements of their songs. The Cassin's Finch song usually is a series of short syllables. The notes are barely separated, giving the song a rushing, warbling sound. Males frequently sing from the tops of conifers. Females occasionally sing (however, recall that first-year males resemble females, so an apparent singing female may be a first-summer male), but their songs are less elaborate than those of males. Their flight call is a distinctive *tidlip* or *krdlii*, whereas that of the Purple Finch is a sharp or hard *pik*.

Similar species   See the account of the Purple Finch.

Geographic variation   Two weakly differentiated subspecies are recognized, *C. c. cassinii* of Idaho and Montana, south to southeastern California and western Texas, and *C. c. vinifer* of southern British Columbia south to northern California. The latter is somewhat larger than the former and has a darker or redder plumage, with a tinge of purple.

Distribution   *Breeds* from the s interior of British Columbia, extreme sw Alberta, n-central and se Montana, n Wyoming, sw South Dakota, and nw Nebraska south (usually from the Cascades eastward) in mountains to e and s California and n Baja California (Sierra San Pedro Mártir), and through w Montana, w Wyoming, w Utah, and Nevada south to n Arizona and n-central New Mexico.

Winters from s British Columbia, nw Montana, and e-central Wyoming south to n Baja California, s Arizona, sw New Mexico, and w Texas, and in the Mexican highlands to Durango, Zacatecas, w San Luis Potosí, and Coahuila, casually to coastal and se California, the Tres Marias Islands (off Nayarit), Michoacán, México, and w-central Veracruz.

Casual north to s coastal Alaska (Middleton Island, Homer), sw British Columbia, se Alberta, and central Texas, and perhaps to North Dakota (sight record).

Conservation status   In appropriate habitat this is an abundant species, suggesting that forestry practices are not deleterious to Cassin's Finches. They also benefit from feeders, and there is no evidence of population declines.

Molt   The First Prebasic plumage is acquired by an incomplete First Prebasic molt that involves body feathers but not remiges or rectrices; males do not acquire red plumage. The Definitive Prebasic molt is complete. Unmated first-year males may start to molt in early July, but older males and females generally do not molt until later in July; the molt lasts two to three months.

Description   **Adult males**—Cap is a bright pinkish red, contrasting with the much paler nape and back, which are washed in pink but streaked brown; ear coverts are often brownish; postocular stripe is bright rose pink; *rump* and uppertail coverts are dull rose pink, streaked with brown; *tail* is brown; *wings* are brownish, with the outer margins of the secondaries slightly pinkish and the tips of the greater and median coverts salmon buff; chin, throat, and breast are bright rose pink, fading to white on the belly and undertail coverts; flanks and undertail coverts have fine brown streaks. **Adult females**—*Head* brownish with a thin, pale eye ring; supercilium and submoustachial streaks pale buff, streaked with thin brown streaks; nape, *back*, and *rump* dusky, streaked with brown; *tail* brown; throat, breast, and flanks whitish, streaked with crisp brown streaks; undertail coverts whitish, thinly streaked with brown. **Juvenal and first-year birds** resemble adult females. *Bill* pale gray, with a dusky tip; *legs* and *feet* pale brownish pink; *iris* dark brown.

Hybrids   No hybrids have been reported.

References   Clement et al. (1993), Hahn (1996), Pyle (1997), Sibley (2000).

31.1 Male Cassin's Finch *Carpodacus cassinii,* Inyo County, California, USA, April 1993. A chunky *Carpodacus* finch that is structurally quite distinct from other members of the genus. Note longish bill with straight culmen, more peaked crown shape, and very long primary extension. Rosy pink on head and breast, brighter red on crown. Note whitish eye crescents and arc below eye. Underparts mostly whitish, with some dusky pink streaking along flanks. The long step between the second and third visible primary tips is distinctive (Larry Sansone).

31.2 Female or First Summer male Cassin's Finch *Carpodacus cassinii,* Mount Pinos, California, USA, July 1999. Most similar to female of eastern form of Purple Finch (see figure 30.2) but note the structural differences, especially the bill shape and long primary extension. The head and body are finely and crisply streaked blackish, giving the bird a clean-cut appearance. Note the whitish eye crescents and pale arc below eye (Brian E. Small).

31.3 Juvenal Cassin's Finch *Carpodacus cassinii*, Jacob Lake, Coconino County, Arizona, USA, August 1999. Similar to adult female, but with warm brown suffusion on head and upperparts and pale cinnamon wing bars. Head pattern less distinct, and streaking somewhat blurrier throughout. Best distinguished from juvenile and female western Purple Finch by bill shape, long primary extension, and less olivaceous plumage (Greg W. Lasley).

31.4 Female or First Basic male Cassin's Finch *Carpodacus cassinii*, Southeast Farallon Island, California, USA, November 1989. A comparative photograph with a female or First Basic male Purple Finch *C. p. californicus* (*left*). Both birds were captured for banding. Note especially the crisp streaking on the head and mantle of the Cassin's Finch as well as the paler edges to the wing coverts and tertials. The long primary extension on the Cassin's Finch is noticeable, especially the long step between the second and third visible primary tips (David D. Beadle).

3 2 **House Finch**

(Carpodacus mexicanus)

Measurements
Length: 12.5–15.0 cm; 4.9–5.9 in.
Wing: 70–83 mm; 2.8–3.3 in. (sexes similar in size).
Mass: 19.0–25.5 g, av. 21.4 g (California).

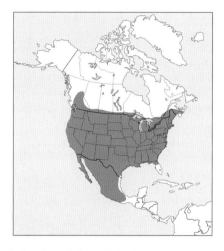

Originally a bird of the Southwest and Mexico, the House Finch was introduced on Long Island, New York, in 1940 and subsequently has spread westward from there as well as eastward from its original range in the Southwest, and now is found throughout the contiguous United States and southern Canada. It is a common urban bird. The bill shape distinguishes it from other *Carpodacus* finches, and the streaking on the flanks differentiates male House Finches from male Purple and Cassin's finches.

Habitat In the West, House Finches occur in arid or semiarid areas, in scrub, brush, oak-juniper woods, chaparral, orchards, farmland, ranges, and suburban areas and villages. In the East, they are principally found in urban areas. They often nest around buildings and even build nests in hanging plants on the balconies of apartments, often several floors above ground. They commonly come to feeders. On the Channel Islands, they usually nest in cholla cactus.

Behavior House Finches are gregarious and generally tolerant of other House Finches. Outside of the breeding season, they often roost in large aggregations, sometimes with House Sparrows. Pair formation begins in winter flocks. At feeders they are aggressive and often are able to displace House Sparrows. Although they are generally resident in the West, migratory behavior apparently has developed in parts of their eastern range. Their flight is undulating, and they hop when on the ground.

Voice The song is a rambling, hoarse warble that shifts rapidly between low and high-frequency notes and characteristically ends with a down-slurred note. In California, the song typically lasts about two seconds and consists of up to about twenty-six syllables. Males occasionally give the song during a butterfly flight display. Females sometimes sing, but female song is not so complex as male song and often is associated with courtship feeding or precopulatory displays. Calls consist of single or multiple *cheep*s, and the flight note is a husky *vweet*.

Similar species See the account of Purple Finch.

Geographic variation Three or four subspecies of House Finches are generally recognized in North America north of Mexico (several additional subspecies are found in Mexico). Geographic variation is moderate but clinal. *C. m. frontalis*, which is resident in southwestern British Columbia east to central Idaho, southeastern Wyoming, and western Nebraska, and south to central Baja California, northwestern Chihuahua, and western and south-central Texas, was introduced into New York and from there has spread throughout the East; it has also been introduced into Hawaii. Some authors recognize *C. m. solitudinus*, which occurs from eastern Washington and Idaho south to southeastern California and northwestern Arizona; males have reduced bright red on their breast. *C. m. clementis*, which is resident on the California Channel Islands, is large billed, has moderately streaked breasts, and males have extensive red (slightly orange) on their breast; apparently they cannot be reliably distinguished from *C. m. frontalis*. *C. m. potosinus*, of southeastern Texas, has heavily streaked underparts, and males have extensive bright red on their breasts.

Distribution *Resident* from sw and s British Columbia (including Vancouver Island; wanders north to n British Columbia and s Alaska [Ketchikan]), n Idaho, Montana, and n-central and se Wyoming east through s Manitoba, central Minnesota, Michigan, s Ontario, sw Quebec (mostly St. Lawrence Valley southward), central New Brunswick, Nova Scotia (absent from Cape Breton Island), and Maine, and south to the Panhandle of Florida, the Gulf Coast, Baja California, Baja California Sur, and in the highlands of Mexico south to central Veracruz, central Oaxaca, and central Chiapas. Some eastern and central (e.g., Manitoba) populations are partially migratory.

Conservation status House Finches are abundant, although they have declined in recent years in the East, probably as a consequence of an eye disease that appears to have killed thousands of finches. By 2002 this disease had spread into the northwestern populations, where it has increased rapidly. In Mexico many House Finches are captured and sold as cage birds, although this practice does not seem to have any significant effect on local populations.

Molt The First Basic plumage is acquired by an incomplete First Prebasic molt that occurs July to October; a variable number of Juvenal remiges are retained. The Definitive Basic plumage is acquired by a complete Prebasic molt, July to October. A limited Prealternate molt has been reported in Arizona.

Description Adult males—Forehead, crown, and malar stripe bright orange red (the red color is affected by the diet, and thus there is a lot of variability, some individuals being more yellowish than red); cheeks and nape grayish, thinly streaked with red; *back* brownish with indistinct dark brown streaks; *rump* and uppertail coverts red; *tail* brown; throat and breast reddish, generally not so bright as the crown; flanks pale with distinct brown streaks; belly and undertail coverts whitish. Adult females—Patterned like males but lacking red. Juvenal and first-year birds (of both sexes) resemble adult females, but juveniles have distinctly buffy tips to some feathers; males attain some red by the first fall. *Bill* grayish, with upper bill darker than mandible; *legs* and *feet* dark brown; *iris* dark brown.

Hybrids House Finches possibly hybridize with Purple Finches.

References Clement et al. (1993), Hill (1993), Pyle (1997), Sibley (2003).

32.1 Male House Finch *Carpodacus mexicanus*, Tucson, Arizona, USA, February 1992. Slimmer than other *Carpodacus* finches, with relatively longer tail, shorter wings, and more rounded head shape. Bill is rather short, with strongly curved culmen. Mostly grayish brown, with reddish crown, throat, and breast. Remaining underparts whitish, with boldly streaked flanks (Rick and Nora Bowers).

32.2 Male House Finch *Carpodacus mexicanus*, Big Bear Lake, San Bernadino County, California, USA, September 2002. In this back view notice the isolated red rump patch, contrasting with the grayish brown, streaky mantle. The grayish brown auriculars separate the reddish crown and throat. Otherwise note the rather rounded head shape and curved culmen on stout bill (Larry Sansone).

32.3 Male House Finch *Carpodacus mexicanus*, Riverside County, California, USA, April 1994. Some male House Finches, including this one, show yellowish or orange crown, throat, and rump instead of red. Such individuals are uncommon, though more frequent than in either Purple or Cassin's finches (Brian E. Small).

32.4 Female House Finch *Carpodacus mexicanus*, Los Angeles, California, USA, October 2002. Rather drab overall. Head and upperparts grayish brown, with indistinct, dusky streaking. Underparts grayish white, streaked dusky along flanks. Wings show narrow pale edges to coverts, forming indistinct wing bars. Best distinguished from other *Carpodacus* finches by structure, bill shape, and relatively plain plumage, especially on head (Brian E. Small).

3 3 Red Crossbill

(Loxia curvirostra)

Measurements
Length: 16–17 cm; 6.3–6.7 in.
Wing: 78–99 mm; 3.1–3.9 in. (males somewhat larger than females; geographically variable).
Mass: 29.2–44.9 g, av 36.5 g (Arizona).

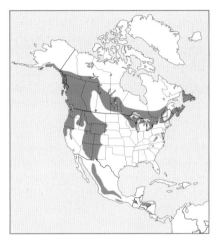

Red Crossbills are medium-sized, chunky finches with distinctive crossed bills that are specialized for opening the scales of conifer cones to extract the seeds, a significant portion of their diet. They are nomadic, appearing in places where there are bumper cone crops of appropriate tree species. Within the species there is a great deal of variation in bill size, reflecting variations in dict: large-billed individuals are specialized to feed on large, hard cones, whereas small-billed birds select small or soft cones. At least eight different flight call types are recognized. In the wild, individuals mate with others with the same call type, and call type and body and bill size are to some degree correlated. The call types do not correlate well with the existing subspecific taxonomy. It has been suggested that the groups defined by body and bill size and call may correspond to different species that are otherwise not separable, and sometimes birds of two different types may be nesting in the same place at the same time, as different species would do. However, molecular differences among the types are slight.

Habitat Red Crossbills are characteristically found in coniferous or mixed woods. They may also be found in suburban situations. Nonbreeding individuals also occur in deciduous woodlands, second growth, weedy fields, and near human habitations.

Behavior Outside of the breeding season, Red Crossbills are gregarious. Although other finches, including Pine Siskins and White-winged Crossbills, may feed with Red Crossbills, they do not stay with them once the flock departs. Red Crossbills often eat salt and gravel from roadsides, where many are killed by traffic. They are easily approached. Most molting takes place from September to December, during which period the birds generally do not nest. Otherwise, nesting seems to take place any time a sufficient cone crop is available. Their flight is strong and rapid, and undulating may occur on short flight. Long flights usually take place high above the canopy. They hop on the ground.

Voice Their song is a series of short, clipped phrases, variously described as *tikuti ti chupity chupity tokit kyip kyip kyip* or *whit-whit, zzzzt, zzzzt, zzzzt, zzzzt*. The flight call, which may be learned during the nestling stage, is generally described as a *chip chip chip* or *kiip kiip kiip*; there are at least eight different call note types, all of which sound, in general, like *chip, kiip, kewp, kyip*, etcetera.

Similar species   The White-winged Crossbill, the only other North American bird with a crossed bill, is different in coloration and has two prominent white wing bars (rarely, Red Crossbills have wing bars). Male White-winged Crossbills are rose red in color, whereas male Red Crossbills are orangish or brick red in color; female White-winged Crossbills have indistinct streaking on the breast and mantle, whereas female Red Crossbills are unstreaked and are dull olive green in color. Juveniles of both species are heavily streaked, but the white wing bars of White-winged Crossbills differentiate them from the Red Crossbills.

Geographic variation   The geographic variation of Red Crossbills is extremely complicated owing to their erratic breeding and nomadism. There is geographic variation in bill size, body size, and flight call type. Most recent workers have divided the North American Red Crossbills into eight types, based on flight call types (Types 1–8). Bill size variation reflects the variation in the size of the cones of conifers that are eaten in different parts of their range and appears to be adaptively labile. For the most part, coloration is not helpful in differentiating among groups. It has been shown that crossbills feed substantially more efficiently on cones that are of a size that is appropriate for their bill: large-billed birds feed efficiently on ponderosa pine or other large-coned pines, and small-billed birds on hemlock or other conifers with small cones. Red Crossbills from the Northwest, where they feed principally on the small cones of hemlock and spruce, are small billed; they also are the smallest in body size of the populations of Red Crossbills. The name *L. c. sitkensis* has been applied to these; they give call Type 3. Crossbills from the Northwest that feed on spruce and Douglas fir, and from the East that feed on spruce, are also relatively small billed and fairly small. The name *L. c. minor* has been applied to the relatively small-billed birds that breed in the East and Southeast, and they also give flight call Type 3. Some crossbills from the Northwest and the East have a similar flight call (call Types 1 and 4). *L. c. percna*, which feeds (or fed—it may be extinct) extensively on black spruce is medium in size with a medium bill length; it also averages darker in color; these are the only crossbills that give Type 8 call notes. *L. c. bendirei, L. c. benti*, and *L. c. grinnelli*, which occur in western pine forests, are of medium size, with a bill of medium size; they feed on pines and spruce, and they are the only crossbills to give Type 5 and Type 7 calls (they also give Type 2 calls). Type 6 calls are given only by the large, large-billed crossbills of southeastern Arizona and the Mexican highlands, which eat pine seeds; the name *L. c. stricklandi* has been used for these birds. Call Types 2, 3, and 4 are widespread in both the East and the West. There are perhaps as many as nine species in North America that differ in morphology and vocalization; in some places two different types breed together, with little or no mixing of types. However, morphological overlap makes it impossible at this time to delimit these groups, and there is a great deal of confusion about which names should be applied to which groups. By definition, different subspecies have different ranges, although often there are zones of intergradation between them, but many crossbill types commonly co-occur geographically; thus, applying subspecific names to these types does not seem to be appropriate. Illustrations of the call types are in the appendix, page 184.

Distribution *Breeds* in both the Old and New Worlds. In North America, breeds from s coastal and se Alaska (west to the base of the Alaska Peninsula and Kodiak Island), s Yukon, s Mackenzie, British Columbia (including Vancouver Island and probably the Queen Charlotte Islands; commonest in se mountains), n Alberta, se Alberta and sw Saskatchewan (Cypress Hills), nw and central Saskatchewan, central Manitoba, central Ontario, s Quebec (few nesting records), Prince Edward Island, Nova Scotia, and Newfoundland south to n Baja California, s California, s Nevada, central and se Arizona, and in the highlands through Mexico, Belize, Honduras, Guatemala, and ne Nicaragua, and in the Rockies and Great Plains region east to se Montana, ne Wyoming, w South Dakota (Black Hills), nw Nebraska, ne and central New Mexico, w Texas (Guadalupe Mountains), and to s Manitoba, ne North Dakota (local elsewhere), n Minnesota, central Wisconsin, central Michigan, s Ontario, Pennsylvania, West Virginia, se New York, and Massachusetts (sporadic; most records from the Berkshire Mountains), and locally in the Great Smoky Mountains in e Tennessee, w North Carolina, and nw Georgia. There isolated breeding records from south of the usual breeding range (s-central Iowa, ne Kansas, Ohio, Arkansas, and e-central Mississippi).

Winters throughout the breeding range, wandering irregularly south to central Baja California (including Cedros and Guadalupe islands), Sinaloa, s and e Texas, n portions of the Gulf states, and casually to s Georgia and central Florida.

Casual in Bermuda and El Salvador, and in summer in the Pribilof and Aleutian islands, and on St. Matthew and St. Lawrence islands in the Bering Sea.

Migrates in nomadic fashion, and may appear throughout the southern part of its breeding range as well as well south of its usual breeding range, especially in the fall and winter. In the fall, the timing of movement corresponds with the times cones open, and large flights are generally seen in May and June, and September and October.

Conservation status Numbers of Red Crossbills are declining, probably principally because of forest fragmentation. Conifers produce substantially more cones after they are at least sixty years old, so large stands of mature conifers are optimal for crossbills. Red Crossbills have been greatly reduced in numbers or possibly extirpated in Newfoundland, apparently because of competition from introduced red squirrels (rare individuals seen in Newfoundland may be wanderers from the mainland). Reducing the amounts of salt and grit used on highways in winter would decrease the number of crossbills killed by traffic.

Molt As a consequence of the variability in nesting season, the timing of the molt is variable. In adults there is a complete molt between April and November. In hatching-year birds there is a partial Prebasic molt from April to December.

Description Adult males—*Head*, mantle, and *underparts* brick red; uppertail coverts blackish brown, tipped with red; *wings* and *tail* blackish brown (rarely has thin, buffy wing bars); undertail coverts grayish white. **First-year males**—Similar to adults but yellowish or orangish yellow instead of red. **Adult females**—Similar to males but olive, yellowish, or gray rather than red; undertail coverts olive gray, with paler margins. **Juveniles**—Heavily streaked, especially ventrally, often yellow washed, and with two faint, dusky wing bars. *Bill* dark, paler at the base; *legs* and *feet* black; *iris* dark brown.

Hybrids   Red Crossbills have been hybridized with White-winged Crossbills in captivity. A natural hybrid between a Red Crossbill and a Pine Siskin has been reported, but the parentage of this specimen has been questioned.

References   Adkisson (1996), Benkman (1993), Clement et al. (1993), Groth (1988, 1993a, b), Marshall et al. (2003), Pyle (1997), Sibley (2000).

33.1 Male Red Crossbill *Loxia curvirostra*, Cabin Lake, Oregon, USA, August 1998. A chunky, large-headed finch with stout bill crossed at tip. Bill size highly variable depending on type (see text). Reddish overall, with grayish cast on mantle, uniform dark wings, and black-streaked, whitish undertail coverts (Brian E. Small).

33.2 Female Red Crossbill *Loxia curvirostra*, Cabin Lake, Oregon, USA, August 1998. Mostly greenish on upperparts, grayer than male on face, and brighter yellow on crown and rump. Underparts yellowish, with pale gray throat and whitish undertail coverts. Note the chunky, short-tailed structure, with rounded head shape and short, strong-looking legs (Brian E. Small).

33.3 Male Red Crossbill *Loxia curvirostra*, Cabin Lake, Oregon, USA, August 1998. Highly variable but generally with a mixture of reddish and yellow green feathers on head and body. This may be a First Summer (second-calendar-year) male, but owing to extensive breeding season and unpredictable molt timing, the aging of many individuals can be difficult. Note short tail, with obvious notch at tip and rather long primary extension (Brian E. Small).

33.4 Juvenal male Red Crossbill *Loxia curvirostra*, Cabin Lake, Oregon, USA, August 1998. Extensively streaked with dusky brown on head and body, with a few red feathers molting in. Wings uniform dark brown, with very narrow pale tips to coverts and tertials (Brian E. Small).

33.5 Juvenal Red Crossbill *Loxia curvirostra*, Estes Park, Colorado, USA, July 2000. Rather pale head and body densely streaked with dusky brown. A few greenish yellow feathers on the rear scapulars and breast indicate this is probably a female. Wings uniform dusky brown, with buffy tips to median and greater coverts forming two even, though very narrow, wing bars (Rick and Nora Bowers).

33.6 Adult male Red Crossbill *Loxia curvirostra*, Jacob's Lake, Arizona, USA, October 2001. This medium-large-billed individual is possibly of the form *Loxia c. grinnelli*, although at this time of year wandering individuals of other forms could possibly occur in this part of Arizona. Away from breeding areas, visual subspecific identification of Red Crossbills, more often than not, is unreliable. Even within an area, more than one form might occur (Larry Sansone).

33.7 Female Red Crossbill *Loxia curvirostra*, Deschultes National Forest, Oregon, USA, September 1994. A medium-billed individual that could be one of several forms occurring in the region. Note that this bird is in active wing molt. The wings feathers are brown and old, with several outer secondaries and inner primaries missing and one blackish new feather appearing in the gap (Larry Sansone).

33.8 Adult male Red Crossbill *Loxia curvirostra*, Cranberry Marsh, Whitby, Ontario, January 2000. A medium-billed individual. Several forms are known to winter in Ontario, making subspecific identification all but impossible without actually hearing the birds call (Sam Barone).

33.9 Adult female Red Crossbill *Loxia curvirostra*, Cranberry Marsh, Whitby, Ontario, January 2000. As with figure 33.8, this individual cannot be reliably assigned to subspecies on visual evidence alone. Wintering birds in Ontario belong to either the medium-billed *"pusilla"* group, which includes the forms *bendirei*, *pusilla* and, *benti*, or the small-billed *"minor"* group, which includes *minor* and *sitkensis* (Sam Barone).

33.10 Adult male Red Crossbill *Loxia curvirostra*, Memorial University of Newfoundland, St. John's, Newfoundland, Canada, April 2002. This bird is most probably of the form *Loxia c. percna*, which is restricted to Newfoundland as a breeding bird and is now rare (David Fifield).

33.11 Female Red Crossbill *Loxia curvirostra*, Memorial University of Newfoundland, St. John's, Newfoundland, Canada, April 2002. As with figure 33.10, this individual is probably of the form *Loxia c. percna*. There are no reliable plumage features to separate this form from any others (David Fifield).

3 4 White-winged Crossbill

(Loxia leucoptera)

Measurements
Length: 14.5–17.0 cm; 5.7–6.7 in.
Wing: 80–93 mm; 3.1–3.7 in. (sexes similar in size).
Mass: Av. ca. 26 g (males slightly heavier than females; little geographic variation).

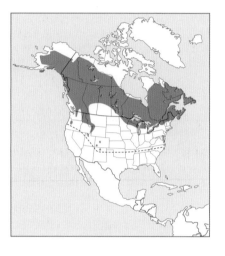

One of the two species of North American crossbills, the White-winged Crossbill is a fairly small crossbill with two conspicuous white wing bars. Males are rosy pink. These birds are nomadic and irruptive, being quite common in some areas one year and virtually absent there the next. In the East, they rarely wander south of the northern states.

Habitat   White-winged Crossbills breed in coniferous forests, especially where rather small-coned species predominate (spruce, fir, larch). In migration and winter, they are also found in deciduous woods, weedy fields, and open conifer plantations. Their white wing bars differentiate them from the only other North American crossbill, the Red Crossbill.

Behavior   White-winged Crossbills typically feed on the seeds of conifer cones, mainly spruce, which they extract while hanging acrobatically from the cone. However, they will also feed on small cones on the ground (e.g., hemlock), and on berries and insects, and their larvae.

Voice   The song is a series of trills on different pitches, *jrrr jrrr jrrr treeeeee kerrrr treeee krrrr* or *trrr tweett tweet tweet trr tchet tchet tweet tweet tweet trrrr tweet tweet*, with the emphasis on the *tweet* elements. Both sexes sing, but males sing much more than females. Song is given while the bird is perched at the top of a tree or when the bird is in a circular display flight. A common flight call is a distinctive *chut-chut-chut-chut* or a nasal *chet-chet-chet*.

Similar species   The Hispaniolan Crossbill (*Loxia megaplaga*) of Hispaniola is larger billed and perhaps more rusty in color. Until recently it was considered to be conspecific. The Two-barred Crossbill of Eurasia is probably also distinct at the specific level, *L. bifasciata*. It is larger, and there are vocal differences between the two. The Red Crossbill is the only other American bird with crossed mandibles. Though Red Crossbills are geographically variable in size, they often are larger than White-winged Crossbills, with the red color of males oranger (male White-winged Crossbills are more of a bright pink, similar to the color of male Pine Grosbeaks); some few Red Crossbills do have two white wing bars, although these are generally not so bold as those of the White-winged Crossbill.

Geographic variation   No geographic variation has been described among North American populations.

Distribution   *Breeds* from w and central Alaska, Yukon (rare in north), n and e-central Mackenzie, n Saskatchewan, Manitoba (rare in south), n Ontario, Quebec, n-central Labrador (north to limit of trees), and Newfoundland south to s Alaska (west to the base of the Alaska Peninsula and Kodiak Island), British Columbia (especially central and s interior), Washington, and ne Oregon (with an isolated populations in the Cascade Mountains; breeding not confirmed), and isolated populations breed irregularly in the mountains of Utah (Summit County), sw Colorado, perhaps Nevada, and probably n-central New Mexico, w Montana, nw and central (Casper) Wyoming, central and sw Alberta, central Saskatchewan, se Manitoba, n Minnesota, n Wisconsin, n Michigan, s Ontario, sw Quebec, central New York, n Vermont, New Hampshire, Maine, New Brunswick, and Nova Scotia.

Winters throughout the breeding range, wandering irregularly and sporadically south to w Washington, n Nevada, central and se Utah, central New Mexico, n Texas (Amarillo, Lubbock), central Oklahoma, Arkansas, Kentucky, Tennessee, Virginia, and North Carolina.

Casual in the Bering Sea (the Pribilofs, St. Lawrence Island, and at sea), coastal British Columbia, s Utah, nw California (one record), n Manitoba, s Baffin Island, and Bermuda.

Conservation status   The coniferous forests in which White-winged Crossbills nest, especially black spruce, are being logged at a rapid rate, and this will decrease habitat suitable for this species. Like Red Crossbills, these birds also pick up salt and grit from along roads, where many are killed by vehicles.

Molt   Little is known about the molts of White-winged Crossbills. The First Basic plumage is acquired by a First Prebasic molt that involves body feathers and lesser and median coverts but not greater coverts or remiges or rectrices. Because the breeding season is not well defined, molting can take place over a long period of time, depending on the year.

Description   Adult males—*Head*, breast, and *rump* pink in late fall and winter; in spring and summer the plumage reddens as a consequence of wear; belly paler and commonly grayish pink; lores dark; *wings* black with two bold white wing bars and white tips to the scapulars; *tail* black, with black undertail coverts tipped with white. **Adult females**—Breast and *rump* grayish green to yellowish olive with indistinct streaks on the *back*, nape, throat, and breast; flanks and belly tan with dusky streaks. **First-year males** have yellow to red (if molted after July) body feathers. **Juveniles** are thinly streaked both on the *underparts* and *back*, with white wing bars. *Bill* black with grayish tomia; *legs* and *feet* black; *iris* dark brown to black.

Hybrids   In captivity, hybrids between Red and White-winged crossbills have been produced.

References   Benkman (1992), Clement et al. (1993), Pyle (1997).

34.1 Male White-winged Crossbill *Loxia leucoptera*, Cranberry Marsh, Whitby, Ontario, Canada, January 2000. Slighter and longer tailed than Red Crossbill, with a distinctly thinner-based bill. Head and body reddish pink, contrasting with blackish lores, scapulars, and boldly marked black and white wings. Note the white bar on the greater coverts widens on the inner edge. Rear flanks gray, with some blurry streaking (Sam Barone).

34.2 Female White-winged Crossbill *Loxia leucoptera*, Whitby, Ontario, Canada, January 2000. Mostly greenish on head and upperparts, with diffuse dusky streaking. Underparts grayish, with greenish wash on breast and blurry darker streaking. Note obvious white wing bars, though the median bar is often hidden by the fluffy breast feathers. The bill is rather slender, though still with the distinctive crossed tip (James Richards).

34.3 First Basic female White-winged Crossbill *Loxia lecoptera*, Thunder Cape, Sibley Provincial Park, Ontario, Canada, October 1990. Mostly grayish brown, paler gray on underparts, and extensively streaked dusky brown on head and body. Wings with bold white tips to median and greater coverts, forming distinct bars. Body plumage rather loose and fluffy. Best distinguished from juvenile Red Crossbill by more slender bill and distinct white wing bars (David D. Beadle).

3 5 Common Redpoll

(Carduelis flammea)

Measurements

Length: 12.5–14.0 cm; 4.9–5.5 in.
Wing: 67–84 mm; 2.6–3.3 in. (sexes similar in size; geographically variable).
Mass: 10.1–15.0 g, av. 13.0 g (Alaska).

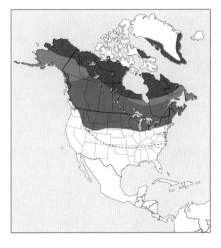

Most of us know the Common Redpoll only as a winter bird, when numbers of them move south, irregularly, into southern Canada and the northern United States. At that time of the year they are almost always found in small flocks, although single birds may be encountered well south of their regular wintering range. They sometimes are found with other species, especially siskins. On the breeding grounds, where they are among the most common songbirds, Common Redpolls are most often associated with birches and willows (the seeds of these trees are an important component of the redpoll diet) at tree line or in open woods. Above tree line they can be found in tall deciduous thickets in sheltered areas. The taxonomy of redpolls is debated—especially their relationship to the closely related Hoary Redpoll.

Habitat   Common Redpolls are found in forested and shrubby areas (commonly willow and birch) and in dwarf woodlands and open tundra. In winter, they occur in a variety of open woodlands, weedy areas, and near human habitations (they often appear at feeders).

Behavior   These redpolls generally are diurnal migrants, although some nocturnal movement has been reported. They usually are found in flocks of fewer than a hundred individuals, but large flocks of thousands of birds have been reported in South Dakota and New Hampshire. Their flight is undulating, and they hop when on the ground. When disturbed, they often fly into a tree or bush, or onto a wire.

Voice   The commonest song is a series of repeated calls, *che che che tschrrrr*. The song is of varied length, can last for nearly half a minute, and uses fourteen to sixteen notes. The commonest call is a short *che*. The rattle call is *tschrrrr*. These redpolls also give a plaintive nasal whistle that rises in pitch.

Similar species   They are similar to Hoary Redpolls, and some consider them to be conspecific. In some areas (e.g., Alaska) "Hoary" and "Common" redpolls seemingly grade into each other, whereas in others (e.g., northern Manitoba) they appear to be more distinct, differing in relative abundance in different years. Many Common Redpolls can appear to have white rumps, especially in flight. Molt may contribute to the confusion about identification. The single molt occurs in late summer, and because the tips of the feathers are pale in color, the redpolls appear to be more pallid at that time than they do in spring and summer, when the feather tips have worn off.

Geographic variation   Two subspecies are generally recognized in North America, *C. f. flammea*, which breeds from Alaska east to Newfoundland, and *C. f. rostrata*, which breeds on Baffin Island, Greenland, and Iceland. *C. f. rostrata* is larger than *C. f. flammea* and has a larger, stouter bill, has more distinct, dusky streaking, is darker (dusky), and is more richly colored than *C. f. flammea*. Male *C. f. rostrata* lack red in the malar area, which male *C. f. flammea* characteristically have.

Distribution   Holarctic in distribution. In North America **breeds** from w and n Alaska, n Yukon, n Mackenzie, s Victoria Island, n Nunavut, n Quebec, Baffin Island, and n Labrador south to the eastern Aleutians (Unalaska), St. Matthew Island (rare; both redpoll species breed there, but many are intermediates), s coastal and se Alaska, nw British Columbia, central Alberta, n (and rarely s) Saskatchewan (possibly in Cypress Hills), n Manitoba, n Ontario, central Quebec (possibly rarely south to 47°N), and Newfoundland (absent in the southwest).

   Winters from central Alaska, southern Mackenzie, n Saskatchewan, n Manitoba, central Ontario, s Quebec, central Labrador, and Newfoundland south to the n United States, irregularly or casually south to w Oregon, n California, n Nevada, n Utah, central Colorado, Kansas, n Oklahoma, Arkansas, n Alabama, and South Carolina.

   Migrates through the Aleutian Islands.

Conservation status   Redpolls are common, and their breeding habitat is found in areas where human activities are minimal. They readily coexist with people and can be found in villages during any time of the year. They are sometimes killed by vehicles, especially when foraging along roadsides. They are not listed as threatened.

Molt   The Juvenal plumage is a acquired by a complete Prejuvenal molt; it is much like the Definitive Basic plumage but fluffier, and juveniles lack red on the crown, rump, or underparts. The First Basic plumage is acquired by a partial First Prebasic molt from July through October and includes body feathers, some or all of the median coverts, some of the inner greater coverts, rarely the eighth secondary and the two inner rectrices. The Definitive Basic plumage is acquired by a complete Prebasic molt, from July through October.

Description   Adult males—Forehead (near bill), lores, and throat blackish; crown bright pinkish red (sometimes orangish or gold); *upperparts* dark grayish brown, streaked with buff; *rump* and uppertail coverts grayish brown and streaked, sometimes washed with pink; *tail* blackish; *underparts* pale buff, with bold streaks on flanks and variable amounts of deep pink on the breast and perhaps belly; malar pink (*C. f. flammea*) or dusky (*C. f. rostrata*); undertail coverts pale with conspicuous blackish streaks. **Adult females**—Like adult males but lacking pink on the breast and malar areas. **First-winter birds**—Like adults, but males probably lack pink or red on their breasts. *Bill* in winter is horn colored at base, dusky at tip, but the bill gets darker in the breeding season; *legs* and *feet* dusky brown; *iris* dark brown.

Hybrids   In some areas, populations of Common and Hoary redpolls seem to grade into each other. It is not clear whether this reflects interbreeding or within-population variation. Also hybrids with the Pine Siskin have been reported.

References Beadle and Henshaw (1996), Knox and Lowther (2000a), Pyle (1997), Seutin et al. (1992), and Troy (1985).

35.1 Breeding male Common Redpoll *Carduelis f. flammea*, Churchill, Manitoba, Canada, June 1998. A small, streaky *Carduelis* finch with a small, pointed bill. On this moderately worn breeding bird note the extensive rose red forecrown, malar patch, and breast. Remaining underparts whitish, with heavy dusky streaking along flanks. Wing bars and edges to mantle feathers have been largely lost because of abrasion. Similar to Hoary Redpoll but slighter, with relatively smaller head and longer, more slender bill. Plumage averages darker overall, with more streaking on underparts (Jim Burns/Natural Impacts).

35.2 Female Common Redpoll *Carduelis f. flammea*, Nome, Alaska, USA, June 1990. Similar to Alternate male but lacks pink or red on face and breast, and shows rather more dusky streaking on sides of breast and along flanks. Head mostly grayish, lightly streaked darker, with red forecrown and black lores and chin. Bill mostly dusky at this time of year. Best distinguished from female Hoary Redpoll by structure, bill shape, and, on average, darker plumage, though much overlap occurs (Brian E. Small).

35.3 Basic male Common Red-poll *Carduelis f. flammea*, Net-cong, New Jersey, USA, January 1994. Similar to Alternate male but, in fresh plumage, paler and cleaner looking with more rosy pink color on malar and breast. Underparts whitish, with dusky streaking confined to flanks and undertail coverts. Bill mostly yellow in winter. Hoary Redpoll of the form *C. f. ex-ilipes* can appear similar but is generally paler overall, with more restricted dark streaking on underparts, and usually lacks obvious dark centers to undertail coverts (Kevin T. Karlson).

35.4 Basic female Common Red-poll *Carduelis f. flammea*, Duluth, Minnesota, USA, February 2004. Similar to Basic male but lacks pink on malar and breast. Lower back and rump whitish, with variable dusky streaking. There is much overlap of features with Hoary Redpoll, though on average Hoary Redpoll tends to be paler overall, with a more distinctly whitish lower back and rump and slightly wider white wing bars and edges to tertials (Laura Erickson).

35.5 Basic female Common Red-poll *Carduelis f. flammea*, Duluth, Minnesota, USA, February 2004. Redpolls can be difficult to age in the field. The shape of the tips of the tail feathers offers a clue here, as the fresh central feathers have rounded tips and the outer feathers appear relatively worn, with more pointed tips. This suggests this is possibly a first-winter bird. On average first-winter birds are extensively brown on nape and mantle with a buffy suffusion to face, breast, and flanks (Laura Erickson).

35.6 Juvenal Common Redpoll *Carduelis f. flammea*, Churchill, Manitoba, Canada, June 1998. Differs from adult birds in lacking red on forecrown and having very bold and dense, dusky streaking on head, breast, and flanks. Note the tiny, pointed bill and narrow, whitish eye crescents (Jim Burns/Natural Impacts).

35.7 First Basic Common Redpoll probably *Carduelis f. rostrata*, Fair Isle, Shetland, UK, October 1996. The Greenland form (*C. f. rostrata*), along with the Islandic form, *C. f. islandica*, are distinctly larger than other Common Redpolls and have larger, deeper-based bills and overall darker brown plumage. Note the extensive buffy brown tones on the head, breast, and flanks and the thick, dusky streaking on mantle and along the flanks (Steve Votier).

35.8 First Basic Common Redpoll, probably *Carduelis. f. rostrata*, Fair Isle, Shetland, UK, October 1996. On this individual notice the deep-based bill and the heavily streaked and rather brown plumage. As with the nominate form of Common Redpoll, the rump is somewhat paler but is heavily streaked blackish (Roger Riddington).

36 Hoary Redpoll

(Carduelis hornemanni)

Measurements
Length: 11.4–14.0 cm; 4.5–5.5 in.
Wing: 67–90 mm; 2.6–3.5 in. (geographically variable).
Mass: 11.4–16.1 g, av. 12.7 g (Alaska).

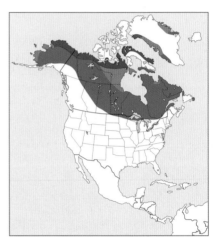

Hoary Redpolls are pale redpolls of the high Arctic of Greenland and northeastern Canada and the low Arctic of central and western Canada and Alaska. The low Arctic birds are particularly variable, and in many places you will find a seeming continuum in coloration between Hoary and Common redpolls. It is not clear whether this represents variability within each group or intergradation between the two. "Typical" adult male Hoary Redpolls are virtually unstreaked below, with few or no streaks on the undertail coverts.

Habitat Hoary Redpolls breed in the high Arctic in shrubby areas and low sparse vegetation in open tundra, or farther south in dwarf trees (birch, willow, and spruce). In migration and winter, they are found in open areas, including open woodlands and fields, and around human habitations.

Behavior An irruptive species, the Hoary Redpoll winters within its breeding range, with only a few birds moving as far south as southern Canada and the northern United States, where they are generally found in flocks of Common Redpolls. In the nonbreeding season, Hoary Redpolls are typically in small, loose flocks. Their flight is undulating, similar to that of the Common Redpoll. They hop on the ground and will flush up into trees or bushes if disturbed.

Voice The vocalizations of Hoary Redpolls are similar to those of Common Redpolls.

Similar species See the account of the Common Redpoll. There are age, sexual, and geographic variations in the taxa of redpolls, confounding their taxonomy. Some authors consider them to be the same species. Others suggest that *C. h. exilipes*, at least, should be included with the Common Redpolls, although the large, pallid redpoll, *C. h. hornemanni*, of northern Greenland and islands in Nunavut may be specifically distinct. In addition to being generally darker and more brightly colored, Common Redpolls generally have distinctly darkly blotched undertail coverts, a streaked rump, and distinct streaking on the flanks. In contrast, *C. h. hornemanni* have unblotched or nearly unblotched undertail coverts, a white rump, and indistinct streaking on the flanks; many *C. h. exilipes*, however, are intermediate.

Geographic variation   Traditionally, two different subspecies of Hoary Redpolls are recognized, the nearly circumpolar *C. h. exilipes* and *C. h. hornemanni*, which breeds in northern Greenland and on Ellesmere, Axel Heiberg, Devon, Bylot, and northern and eastern Baffin islands. *C. h. hornemanni* are the largest of the redpolls, have stubby bills, and are whitish with little dusky streaking, usually restricted to the flanks; on adult males, the pink on the breast is pale. The dusky *C. f. rostrata* of Greenland are nearly as large as *C. h. hornemanni*, whereas *C. h. exilipes* are about the same size as *C. flammea*.

Distribution   Circumpolar. In North America, *breeds* in w and n Alaska (south to Hooper Bay), n Yukon, n and e-central Mackenzie, s Victoria Island, Nunavut, ne Manitoba, Southhampton Island, n Quebec (Kuujjuaq), and n Labrador, and also in nw Greenland and on Ellesmere, Axel Heiberg, Bylot, and n Baffin islands.

   Winters in the breeding range (except in the extreme north) and south, irregularly and sporadically, to s Canada, ne Oregon, Montana, Wyoming, South Dakota, Iowa, Wisconsin, n Illinois, central Indiana, n Ohio, New York, West Virginia, Maryland, and New England. *C. h. hornemanni* winter in s Greenland and casually south to n Manitoba, Nunavut, n Michigan, s Ontario, s Quebec, Labrador, and the British Isles; accidental in central Alaska (Fairbanks).

Conservation status   Habitats in the remote breeding areas of Hoary Redpolls have been little affected by human activities. They are tolerant of humans and may occur in villages at any time of year. They are not considered threatened.

Molt   The Juvenal plumage is acquired by a complete Prejuvenal molt; there is no information on the timing of this molt. The First Basic plumage is acquired by a partial First Prebasic molt that does not include remiges or rectrices; on Baffin Island this molt starts in August. The Definitive Basic plumage is acquired by a complete Prebasic molt, apparently from mid-June through mid-September. Having only an annual molt results in considerable variation in appearance over the course of the year due to feather wear.

Description   **Adult males**—Similar to Common Redpoll but more pallid (esp. *C. h. hornemanni*) and little if any streaking on the *rump* and flanks; malar areas pale, with a rosy wash on the breast. **Adult females**—Like adult males, but with little or no red on the forecrown and lacking the rosy wash on the *underparts*. **First-year birds**—Like adults, but young males probably have less red on their *underparts*. **Bill** varies from horn color to yellowish in winter but turns dark during the breeding season (especially the culmen); *legs* and *feet* blackish; *iris* dark brown.

Hybrids   See the comments in the account of the Common Redpoll.

References   Knox and Lowther (2000b), Pyle (1997), Troy (1985).

36.1 Breeding male Hoary Redpoll *Carduelis h. exilipes*, Nome, Alaska, USA, June 1998. Very similar to Common Redpoll, and there is much overlap of features, but averages paler overall, with a slightly deeper-based, shorter bill. Rather similar to breeding male Common Redpoll but whiter on under-parts, with very faint, narrow streaking on flanks and re-stricted pink flush on breast. Note the bill shape and some-what blocky head, creating a chunkier appearance (Brian E. Small).

36.2 Breeding female Hoary Redpoll *Carduelis h. exilipes*, Nome, Alaska, USA, June 1998. Similar to Alternate male but lacks pink on breast and shows more streaking along flanks. The rear scapulars–lower back–rump area is extensively whitish, with narrow dark cen-ters to feathers. Note also the somewhat bull-necked appear-ance and the deep-based, shortish bill. Female Common Redpoll is, on average, darker overall, with less white on rump, and is more heavily streaked on the flanks (Brian E. Small).

36.3 Breeding female Hoary Redpoll *Carduelis h. exilipes*, Nome, Alaska, USA, June 1998. In this profile the chunky head and neck shape and thick-based bill structure are shown to good effect. Note the pale overall appearance and re-stricted, fine dusky streaking on breast and flanks. The white un-dertail coverts lack obvious dark centers to the feathers. Hoary Redpolls often show rather loose thigh feathers, cre-ating "shaggy trousers." Bill is dusky during breeding season (Brian E. Small).

36.4 Basic female Hoary Redpoll *Carduelis h. exilipes*, Duluth, Minnesota, USA, March 1996. Can appear very similar to Common Redpoll in winter but averages paler overall, especially on rear scapulars and lower back. The underparts are white, with some dusky streaking on sides of breast and along flanks. The undertail coverts appear uniformly white, lacking dark centers to the feathers. Supporting features are the blocky head shape and shaggy thigh feathers (Mike Danzenbaker).

36.5 Definitive Basic male Hoary Redpoll *Carduelis h. hornemanni*, Duluth, Minnesota, USA, February 2004. Subspecific identification of Hoary Redpolls can be tricky, with much individual variation occurring. The large size and very pale plumage of this winter male suggests it is of the Greenland form *Carduelis h. hornemanni*. Compared with the adjacent Common Redpoll (*right*), note the broad white edges to the rear scapulars and lower back and the completely white rump showing a tinge of pink. Note also the wide white bar on the greater coverts and edges to the tertials (Laura Erickson).

36.6 Definitive Basic male Hoary Redpoll, Duluth, Minnesota, USA, February 2004. Another view of the same bird as figure 36.5. Hoary Redpolls often forage on the ground, with tail slightly cocked and wings drooped, thus exposing the whitish rump more clearly. The underparts are white, with restricted and very fine, dark streaking along the flanks. The rounded tips to all the tail feathers indicate this is an adult bird (Laura Erickson).

36.7 Basic Hoary Redpoll, Norfolk, UK, January 1996. Another individual thought to be of the nominate form *Carduelis h. hornemanni.* Note the bull-necked appearance and the short, deep-based bill. The lower back and rump are white, with little or no streaking visible. The underparts are uniformly white, with fine, dusky streaking restricted to the sides of breast and flanks. The buffy suffusion on the head and the amount of streaking on the underparts suggest this may be a bird in First Basic plumage, but aging is often not possible (George Reszeter).

3 7 Eurasian Siskin

(Carduelis spinus)

Measurements
Length: 11.0–12.0 cm; 4.3–4.7 in.
Wing: 69–76 mm; 2.7–3.0 in. (sexes similar in size).
Mass: 10.3–18.5 g, av. 13.6 (England, October).

The Eurasian Siskin is a Palearctic species that is accidental in the Aleutian Islands. Records from other parts of North America may be of escaped cage birds.

Habitat   These birds are found in coniferous woodlands (mainly spruce) and birch and alder thickets. In winter, they wander into urban areas, orchards, and wet riparian groves.

Behavior   Eurasian Siskins principally feed in trees but will forage on the ground on fallen seeds and to pick up grit. In migration and winter, siskins are gregarious, often occurring in large flocks, and they often associate with other *Carduelis* species and sometimes other birds. In North America, however, only single birds are seen.

Voice   The song is a jumbled mixture of finch-like notes, with many twitters, trills, and wheezy notes interspersed. The call is a ringing, tinny *tsuu-ee*.

Similar species   See Pine Siskin. The black head and throat of the Eurasian Siskin male are distinctive, and females are much yellower than female Pine Siskins.

Geographic variation   Although they are widespread in the Palearctic, with widely disjunct western and eastern populations, there is little geographic variation among Eurasian Siskins.

Distribution   *Breeds* from the British Isles and Scandinavia discontinuously across the Palearctic to Siberia, south to s Europe, n Iran, ne China, and Japan.
   Winters in much of the breeding range south to the Mediterranean countries, the Middle East, e China, and the Philippines.
   Accidental in Alaska (Attu Island in the Aleutians, sight record 4 June 1978 and specimen 21–22 May 1993). Also recorded in s Ontario, St. Pierre et Miquelon, Maine, Massachusetts, New Jersey, and Michigan (Whitefish Point), with unconfirmed records from elsewhere; however, these may represent escaped cage birds.

Conservation status   The Eurasian Siskin is extralimital in our area but is locally common in its Eurasian range.

Molt   There is a complete Prebasic molt, July to October.

Description   **Adult males**—Crown, forehead, and throat black; nape and ear coverts green, with yellow supercilium starting at eye and extending behind ear coverts; mantle green, faintly streaked with black; *rump* yellow. **Underparts** yellow green, with black-streaked flanks. Median coverts black, broadly tipped with greenish yellow; primary coverts black, tipped with green; greater coverts black, edged with green; bases of *wing* feathers yellow, forming a yellow stripe in flight. *Tail* short and notched and black, with yellow edge toward base. **Adult females**—Like adult males, but without black on *head* and throat; breast paler than males', heavily streaked with dark brown. *Bill* sharply pointed and brownish horn; lower bill paler; *legs* and *feet* dark brown; *iris* black.

Hybrids   Although Eurasian Siskins interact with Pine Siskins in captivity, no hybrids have been reported.

References   Clement et al. (1993), Cramp and Perrins (1994a).

37.1 Male Eurasian Siskin *Carduelis spinus*, Oxon, UK, 1999. A small, long-winged *Carduelis* finch with a slender, sharply pointed bill. Upperparts greenish, with yellowish rump and boldly patterned black and yellow wings. Head mostly greenish yellow, with contrasting black crown. Throat and breast yellow, merging into whitish belly and undertail coverts. Flanks with bold, blackish streaking. Similar male Pine Siskin has brownish head, lacking Eurasian's black crown and yellow face (George Reszeter).

37.2 Female Eurasian Siskin *Carduelis spinus*, Oxon, UK, February 2000. Notably duller than male, with less yellow on head and breast and more extensive dusky streaking on mantle and underparts. Best distinguished from bright Pine Siskin by yellow highlights on head, breast, and rump and wide yellow wing bars (George Reszeter).

3 8 **Pine Siskin**

(Carduelis pinus)

Measurements
Length: 11.0–13.0 cm; 4.3–5.1 in.
Wing: 66-77 mm; 2.6–3.0 in. (sexes similar is size).
Mass: 10.8–20.1 g, av. 14.6 g (Pennsylvania).

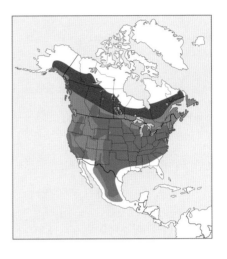

The Pine Siskin is a close relative of the goldfinches, with which it sometimes associates in winter. Siskins generally breed in coniferous or mixed forests. Their bold streaking, especially on the underparts, is distinctive, as is their ascending, buzzy *zree-e-e-e-eet* call. Siskins have thin, pointed bills compared with those of similar finches such as goldfinches and redpolls.

Habitat   Pine Siskins inhabit coniferous (especially spruce) forests, mixed woods, and thickets, and can occur in urban areas. In winter they can be found in open areas, pastures, and lawns, where they feed on grass, dandelion, ragweed, and sunflower seeds; they often come to feeders, where they mix with other *Carduelis* finches. In Massachusetts, nesting frequency seems to have increased in recent years, with a bias for records from areas where feeders abound.

Behavior   Pine Siskins are social at all seasons, and are often seen in flocks that can be large, sometimes with other small finches, especially American Goldfinches. They feed on the seeds of small-coned conifers (e.g., western red cedar) as well as small-seeded deciduous trees, especially alders, and they are often attracted to feeders, especially when nyjer or thistle seed is available. They also glean arthropods (including sawfly and budworm larvae) from bark and from conifer needles. They are attracted to salt along highways. Their flight is undulating. They generally are not seen on the ground, but when there they move in short steps, with occasional hops.

Voice   A common and distinctive call of the Pine Siskin is an ascending *zree-e-e-e-eet* or *zhreeeeee*. Other common calls include *chee-ew* and a bubbly *pip pip pip pip*. The songs are complex and generally given by males in breeding condition. They have been described as a series of husky, whispered trills interspersed with down-slurring notes, rolls, and short rising notes; songs can last over ten seconds.

Similar species   The Eurasian Siskin is similar. It is generally yellower than the Pine Siskin and not so streaked on the underparts; however, some Pine Siskins are quite yellowish with relatively faint streaking (most of these are found in the Southwest);

Eurasian Siskins have a yellowish supercilium, whereas Pine Siskins have an indistinct pale buffy supercilium. Eurasian Siskin males also have a dark crown and chin; they are extralimital in the New World. Female and young Purple Finches are also heavily streaked and often found at feeders. They are larger, chunkier birds with a stout bill (in contrast to the thin, pointed bill of siskins). A number of sparrows are streaked, but they lack yellow wing bars and yellow at the sides of the base of the tail (female and young siskins are often not noticeably yellow). Sparrows are behaviorally much different, commonly foraging on the ground and rarely associating with finches, whereas siskins are only occasionally seen on the ground and are often with other finches, especially *Carduelis* finches.

Geographic variation   Geographic variation is slight and is obscured by variation within populations. Nonetheless, three subspecies have been recognized, *C. p. pinus*, which breeds from Saskatchewan east to Newfoundland, *C. p. vagans*, which breeds from Alaska east to Alberta, and *C. p. macroptera*, which breeds in Mexico and has been reported as a wanderer to Arizona and New Mexico. *C. p. macroptera* is larger than the other two (wing length 70–80 mm, cf. 66–77 mm). It has indistinct, dusky ventral streaking and, on average, more extensive yellow in the bases of the flight feathers. *C. p. pinus* is the darkest of three, with dense, black streaking on the underside, whereas *C. p. vagans* is intermediate in coloration.

Distribution   *Breeds* from central (where very rare) and s coastal Alaska, central Yukon, sw Mackenzie, nw, w, and n Alberta, and e-central Saskatchewan, se Alberta and sw Saskatchewan (Cypress Hills), central Manitoba, central Ontario, and Quebec (north to 51°N), s Labrador, and Newfoundland south in the West to s-central California through w Washington and w and ne Oregon (Wallowa, Blue, and Steens mountains), Nevada (absent in the southwest), n and e Arizona, w New Mexico, and w South Dakota (Black Hills), and in the East to n Minnesota, n Wisconsin, n Michigan, s Ontario (absent in the southwest), central Maine, ne New York, n Vermont and New Hampshire, and Massachusetts (increasing?), and in the highlands of Mexico and Central America in ne Baja California (Sierra San Pedro Mártir), e Sonora, central Durango south to Puebla, and locally in Chiapas and Guatemala; erratic.

   Winters throughout its breeding range but principally in the southern part, and irregularly into central Baja California, n Sonora, n Veracruz, and throughout the Gulf states and occasionally to n Florida. Vagrant in winter to s Baja California Sur (Cape Region).

   Rare in fall in central British Columbia. **Casual** or accidental in the Shumagin Islands, the Pribilofs, and e Aleutians (Unimak and Unalaska islands), on St. Lawrence Island in the Bering Sea, in n Alaska (Nuvagapak Point, Point Barrow, Chandler Lake, Brooks), on Bathurst, Cornwallis, and Coats islands, in n Manitoba, and on Bermuda.

Conservation status   Clearing of coniferous and mixed forests has undoubtedly led to a decrease in the numbers of Pine Siskins, but small clear-cuts may be beneficial to them, as areas with forest edge often support larger populations than continuous forest. They frequently gather along roadsides, where they eat salt and grit, and many are killed by traffic. Overall, however, this is a common species, not in immediate danger.

Molt   The First Basic plumage is acquired by a partial First Prebasic molt; this molt includes the body plumage but not the remiges or rectrices; it commences in August and may continue into October. There is no Alternate plumage. The Definitive Basic plumage is acquired by a complete Definitive Prebasic molt beginning in August.

Description Adult males—*Head* brown, with thin brown streaking on the side of neck and nape and dark streaking on the *back*. *Tail* brown, with yellow in the basal two-thirds of the lateral rectrices; *underparts* whitish, with bold, crisp brown streaks. *Wings* dark brown with broad yellow tips to the greater coverts, forming a broad, yellow wing bar; the tips of the lesser coverts have narrow white tips, forming a thin wing bar. In flight a broad yellow wing stripe is visible from both above and below. **Adult females**—Resemble adult males but often have less (or no) yellow. **First-winter birds** resemble adults, except that their rectrices are less truncate. **Juvenile birds** are somewhat darker and buffier than birds in Basic plumage. *Bill* of juveniles is pinkish buff; that of adults is dusky or blackish, often bluish at the base of the lower mandible; *legs* and *feet* of juveniles are pinkish and those of adults vary from dark brown to dark horn color or even dusky; *iris* brown.

Hybrids Pine Siskins are known to hybridize with Red Crossbills and Common Redpolls.

References Dawson (1997), Howell and Webb (1995), Kessel and Gibson (1978), Peterson and Meservey (2003), Pyle (1997).

38.1 Male Pine Siskin *Carduelis pinus*, Portal, Arizona, USA, May 1999. A small, long-winged *Carduelis* finch with a slender, sharply pointed bill. Head and upperparts brownish, densely streaked dusky black. Underparts off-white, with dense blackish streaking on breast and along flanks. Wings blackish, with bold pale yellow tips to greater coverts and bright yellow edges to primaries, forming a patch at the base of inner primaries. Could be confused with Common Redpoll in winter, but note distinctive bill shape, yellow in wings, and lack of red forecrown (Brian E. Small).

38.2 Female Pine Siskin *Carduelis pinus*, Portal, Arizona, USA, May 1999. Similar to male, but with whitish tips to greater coverts and with less yellow on edges of primaries, without patch at base of inner primaries. Note the densely streaked underparts, including the undertail coverts. Differs from other *Carduelis* finches by very streaky appearance and bill shape. Similar to female Eurasian Siskin but lacks yellow tones on head and breast, has more extensively streaked underparts and whitish wing bars (Brian E. Small).

38.3 First Basic Pine Siskin *Carduelis pinus*, Kitchener, Ontario, Canada, January 2004. The general appearance of this species remains much the same year-round. This individual shows some contrast between the retained Juvenal outer greater coverts, worn and brown, with abraded pale tips, and the fresh, blackish-centered remaining feathers. In addition, the primary coverts appear rather worn, with pointed tips. A winter adult would not be expected to display these molt limits. Many birds cannot be reliably sexed, but the yellowish tips to the inner greater coverts and edges to the flight feathers hint this is a young male (Sam Barone).

38.4 Juvenal Pine Siskin *Carduelis pinus*, Estes Park, Colorado, USA, July 2000. Similar to adult but note extensive buffy brown wash to mantle and scapulars and relatively wide buff tips to median and greater coverts. Best distinguished from other streaky finches by longish, slender, and sharply pointed bill and yellowish flash on flight feathers and base of tail (Rick and Nora Bowers).

39 **Lesser Goldfinch**

(Carduelis psaltria)

Measurements
Length: 7.6–11.0 cm; 3.0–4.3 in.
Wing: 57–69 mm; 2.2–2.7 in. (sexes similar in size).
Mass: 8.0–11.5 g, av. 9.5 g (California).

The Lesser Goldfinch is a small goldfinch of the Southwest. It is not generally so common as the American Goldfinch or as widespread, and its biology is less well known. Interestingly, the males occur in two color forms, a black-backed form in the eastern part of their range and a green-backed form farther west (see subspecies under **geographic variation**). The breeding males of either type are easily identified, but the females are rather nondescript, although more greenish in hue than other female goldfinches.

Habitat   Lesser Goldfinches are found in open woodlands, woodland edges, open fields, pastures, and around human habitations. They feed in trees or shrubs but most commonly on the ground. They readily come to feeders.

Behavior   Like all goldfinches, Lesser Goldfinches are rather gregarious, and they even nest in loose colonial groups, defending territories in the general vicinity of the nest. They are apparently nonmigratory over most of their range, but in winter populations withdraw southward from the coldest parts of their range. In winter, they are often found in mixed flocks of other goldfinches as well as siskins and House Finches and some nonfinch species (e.g., Lark and White-crowned sparrows and Western Bluebirds). Their flight, like that of other goldfinches, is undulating, and although rarely on the ground, they hop when there.

Voice   A common call is a distinctive high, clear, and plaintive *thleee* or *teeeyee*. Their flight call is a harsh, grating *chig-chig-chig* or *chup-chup-chup*. The song is variable and incorporates much mimicry, although less than in Lawrence's Goldfinch. It is slow and disjointed, and there is less repetition than in the song of the American Goldfinch.

Similar species   The Lesser Goldfinch is smaller than the other goldfinches, although this may not be apparent in the field except in mixed flocks. The females are decidedly greenish and generally have at least some white in the base of their primary wing feathers. The white patch in the wings is conspicuous in flying individuals, especially males. For more details on distinguishing the goldfinch species see the account of the American Goldfinch.

Geographic variation   Two well-marked subspecies from north of Mexico are generally recognized. *C. p. psaltria* is largely resident from central-eastern Arizona, northern Colorado, northwestern Oklahoma, and northern and central Texas south through central, eastern, and southern Mexico to Guerrero, Oaxaca, and central Veracruz. *C. p. hesperophilus* is resident from southwestern Washington, western Oregon, southeastern Oregon, northeastern California, northern Nevada, and northern Utah south through California and central Arizona to southern Baja California and southern Sonora. The back and ear coverts of *C. p. psaltria* are olive, mottled with black (rarely completely black); the back and ear coverts of *C. p. hesperophilus* are olive, lacking black. The molt sequences differ (see below).

Distribution   *Resident* from sw Washington, w Oregon (Willamette Valley), e Oregon (Klamath County), n California, s Idaho (rare but perhaps expanding), North Dakota (very rare; black backed), n Utah, s Wyoming (possibly), sw and central Colorado, and w Oklahoma south to s Baja California, through Central America (including Belize), and in South America in Colombia, n Venezuela, w Ecuador, and nw Peru. Some individuals from northern populations move south in winter.

Casual or accidental in British Columbia, Montana, se Colorado, sw South Dakota, Nebraska, Kansas, Missouri (Kansas City), Arkansas, s Louisiana (Cameron, Gretna), Kentucky (Elizabethtown), and Maine (Georgetown); reported in North Dakota, s Ontario, and North Carolina.

Conservation status   There has been a statistically significant long-term decline in the numbers of Lesser Goldfinches throughout their range in the United States, perhaps reflecting habitat loss. They were either overlooked or not present in Oregon in the nineteenth century. Thus, if not overlooked, they have expanded their range northward in the Northwest in the past hundred years.

Molt   There are substantial differences between the molts of the two subspecies, which are discussed separately:

C. p. psaltria has two molts per year, a Prebasic molt in the late fall and a Prealternate molt in the spring. Both molts involve all of the body feathers and some of the remiges and rectrices of both sexes. The First Basic plumage is acquired by the First Prebasic molt, during which all of the body plumage is replaced as well as a variable number of remiges and rectrices; this molt occurs from August through January. The First Prealternate plumage is acquired by a nearly complete Prealternate molt, during which all of the body feathers and (usually) rectrices are replaced and most of the remiges (inner primaries and outer primaries are more likely to be retained); this molt takes place from April to June. The Definitive Basic molt is acquired by a Definitive Prebasic molt that involves all of the body feathers and a variable number of rectrices and remiges; this molt occurs from October to February. The Definitive Prealternate molt is nearly complete and takes place in spring.

C. p. hesperophilus acquires its First Basic plumage by a First Prebasic molt that involves all of the body plumage and a variable number of remiges and rectrices; this molt occurs from May to November. In this race there is little evidence of any Prealternate molt. The Definitive Basic molt is complete and occurs from July to December.

Description   *C. p. hesperophilus*. **Adult males**—Cap black; ear coverts, nape, and mantle greenish yellow; ***tail*** black with large white patches in the lateral rectrices that do not extend to the tip of the tail; ***underparts*** yellowish, with whitish yellow undertail coverts; *wings* black with narrow white tips to the median coverts and broad white tips to the greater coverts, forming two white wing bars; white on the bases of all but the outermost primaries. **Adult females**—Like adult males but with no black on the *head*; *tail* dark brown with little white; *wings* like males' but not so dark. Some females are quite yellowish, whereas others are paler. **First-winter individuals** resemble adult females, but first-winter males may have some black in the cap.

C. p. psaltria. **Adult males**—Cap, ear coverts, nape, *back*, and *tail* black; *underparts* bright yellow; *wing* black, with white tips to the greater coverts and white bases on all but the outermost primaries.

Bill dark brownish, but in males often pinkish brown and grayer at the tip and greenish yellow at the base of the mandible; *legs* and *feet* dark brown to gray brown; *iris* dark brown.

Hybrids   The Lesser Goldfinch has been reported to hybridize with the American Goldfinch.

References   Clement et al. (1993), Marshall et al. (2003), Pyle (1997), Watt and Willoughby (1999).

39.1 Definitive Alternate male Lesser Goldfinch *Carduelis p. psaltria*, Concan, Texas, USA, May 1999. A small and compact *Carduelis* finch with a short, relatively deep-based bill. Black upperparts, wings, and head and uniform yellow underparts create a bicolored appearance. Wings show white bar on greater coverts, patch at base of primaries, and edges to tertials. Bill mostly dusky (Brian E. Small).

39.2 Definitive Alternate male Lesser Goldfinch *Carduelis p. hesperophilus*, Kino Springs, Arizona, USA, August 2001. Differs from the form *C. p. psaltria* by having greenish mantle and auriculars. Note the solidly black crown and the large white patch at the base of the primaries. On this adult bird there is no contrast between the primary coverts and the greater coverts, with all feathers of similar age and tone (Kevin T. Karlson).

39.3 Female Lesser Goldfinch *Carduelis p. hesperophilus*, Kino Springs, Arizona, USA, August 2001. Similar to male but lacks black crown and shows much less white at base of primaries. Face and underparts variably pale yellow, paler on belly. Best distinguished from female American Goldfinch by smaller size, gray, relatively deeper-based bill, and at least some white at the base of the primaries (Kevin T. Karlson).

39.4 Female Lesser Goldfinch *Carduelis p. hesperophilus*, Kern County, California, USA, April 2002. A bright early spring individual. Note the grayish green upperparts, greenish face, and pale yellow underparts. Wings rather dusky, with narrow pale tips to median and greater coverts and whitish edges to tertials. Compared with a bright female American Goldfinch, notice the darker gray bill, small white flash at the base of the primaries, and yellowish undertail coverts (Brian E. Small).

39.5 First Alternate male Lesser Goldfinch *Carduelis p. hesperophilus*, Kern County, California, USA, April 2002. Differs from adult male in having a mixed black and green crown. Note the contrast between the retained, rather worn and brown primary coverts, visible secondaries, and inner primaries and the replaced and blacker-centered coverts, tertials, and outer primaries (Brian E. Small).

Lawrence's Goldfinch

(Carduelis lawrencei)

Measurements
Length: 10.0–11.5 cm; 4.0–4.5 in.
Wing: 62–72 mm, av. 66.1 mm; 2.4–2.8 in. (males slightly larger than females).
Mass: 8.5–12.0 g; male av. 10.2 g; female av. 10.1 g (California).

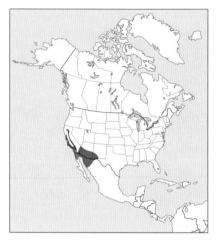

As a breeding bird, Lawrence's Goldfinch is limited in distribution to California and northern Baja California, and even there the species' occurrence is sporadic. Its wintering range also varies from year to year; in many years Lawrence's Goldfinch is found only in southern California and northern Baja California, but sometimes these goldfinches wander as far east as extreme western Texas, and into central Sonora. In all plumages they are the grayest of the goldfinches, and juveniles are the only goldfinches with a conspicuously streaked breast and with brown streaks on the cap. Adult males have conspicuous yellow patches on their wings, which distinguish them from other goldfinches. Their black tail has subterminal white patches formed by white inner webs of all but the central two tail feathers, white underwing coverts, and white undertail coverts—features seen from the underside when they are in flight that aid in their identification.

Habitat   Lawrence's Goldfinches are found in dry, open oak woodlands, chaparral, and piñon-juniper woodlands, often near water. They tend to be found in drier areas than other goldfinches.

Behavior   Lawrence's Goldfinches are gregarious during all seasons, and in winter they may flock with other goldfinches. They sometimes nest in loose colonies, and territories are only weakly defended. Their flight is undulating, and they hop when foraging on the ground. Lawrence's Goldfinches frequently go to water to drink and bathe.

Voice   The song of Lawrence's Goldfinches is similar to that of other goldfinches but is more musical, higher, and tinkling (like wind chimes). Males also mimic, incorporating songs and calls from other species into their song. The flight call is a bell-like *tink-ul* or *ti-too*, and the call is a soft *chee* or nasal *kee-yerr*.

Similar species   Adult males are unmistakable: their black face and crown, their pale gray sides of face, nape, and mantle, and the yellow patch on the wings distinguish them from all other goldfinches. Adult females are much grayer than other goldfinches, and they have two pale yellow or whitish wing bars. Juveniles are streaked below and on their crown. See also the account of the American Goldfinch.

Geographic variation   No geographic variation has been described.

Distribution   *Breeds* from n-central (rarely nw) California south (west of the Sierra Nevada) to s California and n Baja California. Probably breeds casually in s Arizona (juvenile at a feeder in June, Gisela, Gila County).

   Winters from n-central California, s Nevada, central Arizona, and sw New Mexico (irregular) rarely east to w Texas and south to extreme nw Chihuahua, central Sonora, and central Baja California.

   Casual in Oregon (Jackson and Lane counties) and rare on the Channel Islands.

Conservation status   Lawrence's Goldfinches have probably benefited from non-intensive grazing, which probably increases the abundance of some of their favorite food plants. Because their range is so limited, they could be vulnerable to the loss of dry oak woodlands.

Molt   The First Basic plumage is acquired by a partial First Prebasic molt that takes place on the breeding grounds, August to October; it usually includes all body feathers, median and greater coverts, none to all of the rectrices, sometimes inner primaries and outer secondaries, and sometimes tertials. The First Alternate plumage is acquired by a partial First Prealternate molt and usually includes all body feathers and perhaps some greater wing coverts and tertials; this molt occurs in March and April. The Definitive Basic plumage is acquired by a complete molt that occurs July to October; it takes place mostly on the breeding grounds. The Definitive Prealternate molt is similar to the First Prealternate molt.

Description   **Adult males**—Center of the throat and the chin, lores, forehead, and crown are jet-black; nape, ear coverts, *back*, and uppertail coverts, sides of throat, breast, flanks, and belly are pale gray; *rump*, center of the breast, and sometimes the upper belly are washed with yellow; *wing* black, with lesser and median coverts yellow with indistinct gray base; greater coverts with dark bases and broad yellow tips, forming two conspicuous yellow wing bars; primaries and secondaries dark, with yellow outer webs; tertials with pale edges; undertail coverts white; *tail* dark with subterminal white patches on all but the central two rectrices. **Adult females**—Patterned like adult males but have a dusky, not black, face, and are generally duller in coloration. **First-winter males** have a black face but otherwise resemble adult females. **First-winter females** are similar to adult females; greater and median coverts are yellowish, contrasting with the duller primary coverts. **Juveniles** are more brownish and streaked on the crown and *underparts* with diffuse, dull brown streaks. *Bill* flesh colored; *legs* and *feet* dull pinkish; *iris* dark brown.

Hybrids   No hybrids involving this species have been reported.

References   Clement et al. (1993), Davis (1999), Pyle (1997), Russell and Monson (1998).

40.1 Definitive Alternate male Lawrence's Goldfinch *Carduelis lawrencei*, Panoche Road, California, USA, April 1996. A medium-sized *Carduelis* finch with a relatively long tail. Male has unique pattern of pale gray body and head, with contrasting black crown and foreface and yellow breast. Wings with large yellow panels on greater coverts and flight feathers and with pale gray edges to black-centered tertials. Confusion with other goldfinches is unlikely (Mike Danzenbaker).

40.2 Definitive Alternate male Lawrence's Goldfinch *Carduelis lawrencei*, San Bernadino County, California, USA, July 2002. By midsummer a combination of abrasion and sun bleaching can cause even the most handsome of finches to appear rather tatty. This bird has lost much of the yellow and gray feather edges to the coverts and tertials and appears patchy on the body and head plumage (Larry Sansone).

40.3 Female Lawrence's Goldfinch *Carduelis lawrencei*, Mount Pinos, California, USA, July 1994. Similar to male but lacks black on head and has a brownish cast to head and mantle. Underparts pale gray, with a wash of pale yellow on breast. Wings show reduced yellow on coverts but primaries edged bright yellow like male's. Bill grayish. Best distinguished from other *Carduelis* finches by combination of mostly brownish gray plumage and yellow-edged primaries (Brian E. Small).

40.4 Juvenile Lawrence's Goldfinch *Carduelis lawrencei*, San Bernadino County, California, USA, July 2002. Similar to female and likewise has brownish cast to plain head and mantle. Underparts pale gray, washed with brown on breast, and with diffuse, blurry streaking across breast. Wing coverts and tertials tipped pale gray and edged yellowish olive. Note bright yellow edges to primaries. Sexes similar (Larry Sansone).

4 I American Goldfinch

(Carduelis tristis)

Measurements

Length: 11.5–14.0 cm; 4.5-5.5 in.

Wing: 64–81 mm; 2.5–3.2 in. (Ontario) (males somewhat larger than females).

Mass: 14.5 g (January), 11.6 g (September) (Ontario).

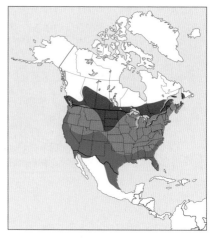

The American Goldfinch, an abundant and widely distributed species, is one of the most familiar songbirds in North America. The breeding males are bright yellow, with a black forehead, forecrown, and wings, whereas females are duller in color with a greenish yellow or (in winter) brownish back. In flight, the white underwing coverts of both males and females may be seen. American Goldfinches are sexually dimorphic in appearance and also vary (unlike most finches) seasonally. In some plumages they can be difficult to distinguish from the other American goldfinches, Lawrence's and Lesser.

Habitat American Goldfinches are found in weedy fields, in open deciduous, mixed, and riparian woodlands, in orchards, and on farmland. In the West, they breed mainly in willows. Goldfinches feed in trees or on the ground and commonly visit feeders.

Behavior The diet of goldfinches consists almost entirely of seeds, particularly those of thistles and other species in the sunflower family. However, they also will feed on small insects and the seeds of small-seeded trees, especially birch and alder. They have a distinctive undulating flight, and when feeding on the ground they hop. In winter, they often are found with siskins and other goldfinches and commonly come to feeders; they are particularly attracted to sunflower seeds and nyjer.

Voice Their song is variable, musical, and sustained: *toWEE toWEE toWEEto tweer tweer tweer*. The flight call is a light, musical, rolling *potato-chip* or *yip-yip*.

Similar species All male goldfinches in breeding plumage are distinctive, but females and young birds can be confusingly similar. Breeding female American Goldfinches are yellowish, with a yellowish olive back, two bold wing bars, and a pinkish bill. Female Lesser Goldfinches are smaller (not always obvious) and yellowish green, with a stout, dark bill and white at the base of the primaries; they have white on the lateral tail feathers that goes all the way to the tip (white on the tail feathers of Lawrence's Goldfinch stops before the tip). Female Lawrence's Goldfinches are grayish, whitish around the eye, with a yellow wash on the belly, broad, yellowish gray wing bars, yellow outer edges to the primaries, and whitish edges to the primaries and the tertials.

Adult females and first-winter birds are like breeding females but with buffy, not whitish, wing bars and tips to the tertials (American). Lesser Goldfinches have yellowish or whitish wing bars. Juvenile Lawrence's Goldfinches have a streaked crown and are heavily streaked below; no other goldfinch is so obviously streaked, and the streaking on Pine Siskins is generally much bolder.

Juvenile American Goldfinches are buffy rust in hue, especially on their belly and undertail coverts, with buffy wing bars. Juvenile Lesser Goldfinches, in addition to being smaller, are more greenish and have a yellowish throat and undertail coverts (unlike Lawrence's Goldfinches).

Geographic variation   Four subspecies of American Goldfinches have been described. Eastern goldfinches (*C. t. tristis*) are brighter in coloration than many western ones: males in Alternate plumage are bright yellow with extensive black on their crown; Basic-plumage birds and females have little olive or gray and are medium brown in color. There are three western subspecies, *C. t. jewetti*, which breeds from southwestern British Columbia south to southwestern Oregon, *C. t. salicamans*, which breeds in western California (west of the Sierra Nevada) south to northwestern Baja California, and *C. t. pallida*, which breeds from south-central British Columbia, central Alberta, central Saskatchewan, southern Manitoba, and extreme western Ontario south to eastern Oregon, central Nevada, central Utah, western Colorado, and extreme northwestern Nebraska. *C. t. pallida* are relatively large; females and individuals in Basic plumage are pale brown with a gray tinge, and Alternate-plumage males are pale yellow with reduced black in the cap. *C. t. salicamans* are like *C. t. pallida* in color but smaller (wing length 62–74 mm; cf. 68–79 mm). *C. t. jewetti* are also relatively small, but females and individuals in Basic plumage are dull brown with an olive tinge, and males in Alternate plumage are bright yellow, but with less black in the cap than *C. t. tristis*.

Distribution   *Breeds* from central (probable; rare) and s British Columbia (including Vancouver Island), n-central Alberta, central Saskatchewan, central and se Manitoba (one record for n Manitoba [Churchill]), s and central Ontario, central Quebec (Anticosti Island [rare] and north to La Sarre, Chibougamau, and Lac Saint-Jean, and east to Sept-Îsles), New Brunswick, Nova Scotia, and sw Newfoundland south to s California (along the coast), nw Baja California (rare), ne California, e Oregon, central Nevada, central Utah, sw and e Colorado, Kansas, Oklahoma (absent in Panhandle and sw), extreme ne Texas, n Louisiana, central Mississippi, central Alabama, central Georgia, w South Carolina, and North Carolina (except in the southeast).

Winters from Washington, s British Columbia, s Manitoba (erratic and uncommon), w and central Montana, Wyoming, central and e Nebraska, c Minnesota, Wisconsin, Michigan, s Ontario, s Quebec, central Maine, central New Brunswick, and s Nova Scotia south to central Baja California, central Sonora, nw Chihuahua, central Coahuila, and e Mexico south to central Veracruz, and to the Gulf Coast and Florida.

Migrates throughout the United states and s Canada.

Conservation status   Although the American Goldfinch remains a common bird, breeding bird survey data show that its numbers have declined in some parts of its range (e.g. Oregon), perhaps because of the use of agricultural chemicals.

Molt   The First Basic plumage is acquired by a partial First Prebasic molt, mid-September through early January, that involves all body feathers but not remiges and rectrices or greater and secondary and (usually) median coverts. There is a partial First Alternate plumage from mid-March through mid-June that involves most body feathers; the Juvenal remiges, rectrices, and coverts are retained. The Definitive Basic plumage is acquired by a complete Definitive Prebasic molt, mid-September through mid-December. The goldfinches are unique among the finches by having an extensive Prealternate body molt in the spring.

Description   **Adult males**—Forehead and forecrown jet-black; remiges black, with white margins on the innermost secondaries and tips of greater coverts; white on the outer webs of the tips of the rectrices, and white underwing coverts and ***rump***; otherwise lemon yellow. ***Males in winter***: brownish gray (no black on ***head***) but yellowish on crown, and white-tipped greater coverts and yellow lesser coverts; remiges black, with whitish tips to primaries and outer webs of secondaries and tertials; in winter, some individuals have a conspicuously whitish ***rump***. **Adult females**—In summer, yellowish gray above and yellowish below, with a yellow throat and belly; wing bars yellowish or white. **Females in winter**: like summer females but grayer, with bold yellow lesser coverts and white tips to greater coverts, narrow white tips to primaries and outer webs of secondaries and tertials. **First-winter birds** are dull rusty yellow on the ***head*** and back, with buff wing bars and outer webs of the secondaries, and edges and tips to the tertials, and lighter rusty ***underparts***. ***Bill*** varies seasonally and is dark grayish brown in winter, often with a darker tip, and brighter in the breeding season, especially in males, which have a yellowish bill; ***legs*** and ***feet*** also change seasonally and are grayish brown in winter, buff or pinkish in summer; ***iris*** dark brown.

Hybrids   American Goldfinches have been reported to hybridize with Lesser Goldfinches.

References   Clement et al. (1993), Marshall et al. (2003), Middleton (1993), Pyle (1997), Rising (2002), Sibley (2000).

41.1 Definitive Alternate male American Goldfinch *Carduelis t. tristis*, Jamestown, North Dakota, USA, June 2002. A medium-size and rather compact *Carduelis* finch with a stout bill. Head and body mostly rich golden yellow, with contrasting black forecrown and white undertail coverts. Wings mostly black, with bright yellow lesser coverts and narrow white edges to greater coverts and tertials. Bill pinkish orange. Virtually unmistakable in this plumage (Brian E. Small).

41.2 Definitive Alternate male American Goldfinch *Carduelis tristis*, Albany, New York, USA, June 2002. In this underside view note how the yellow breast and belly merges into the white undertail coverts. The outer tail feathers show extensive white on the inner webs. Otherwise the black crown and pink bill are distinctive (Kevin T. Karlson).

41.3 Definitive Alternate female American Goldfinch *Carduelis tristis*, Jamestown, North Dakota, USA, June 2002. Duller than male, lacking black forecrown and with greenish mantle, crown, and auriculars. Underparts yellow, with greenish wash across breast and with white undertail coverts. Blackish wings show narrow white tips to coverts and tertials. Best distinguished from similar Lesser Goldfinch by larger size, lack of white at base of primaries, and pinkish orange bill (Brian E. Small).

41.4 Basic male American Goldfinch *Carduelis tristis*, Inyo County, California, USA, November 1996. Rather drab olive gray overall, lacking solid black forecrown. Face tinged greenish, and throat quite bright yellow. Wings mostly black, with yellow lesser coverts (just visible here) and broad whitish tips to greater coverts, tertials, and secondaries. Uniform blackness of primary coverts and greater coverts indicates this is an adult bird (Larry Sansone).

41.5 Basic female American Goldfinch *Carduelis tristis*, Orono, Ontario, Canada, March 1989. Similar to Basic male but even duller, usually lacking extensive yellow on throat. Bill dusky in winter. Best distinguished from other goldfinches by larger size and lack of prominent white or yellow on edges of primaries (James Richards).

41.6 Basic female American Goldfinch *Carduelis tristis*, Inyo County, California, USA, November 1996. A brighter individual than shown in figure 41.5. Best distinguished from Basic-plumaged male by dusky ground color to wings, with no yellow visible on lesser coverts, although these feathers are often mostly hidden, as here, and this feature is hard to see (Larry Sansone).

42 European Goldfinch

(Carduelis carduelis)

Measurements
Length: 12–15 cm; 4.7–6.0 in.
Wing: 73.0–87.5 mm; 2.9–3.4 in.
Mass: 13.0–19.5 g (eastern Netherlands, Germany, all year; males slightly heavier than females).

Although the European Goldfinch has been introduced several times in North America (Massachusetts, New York, New Jersey, Pennsylvania, Ohio, Missouri, Oregon), it is not presently established in any of these places. The numerous sightings of this species are probably based on birds that have escaped from captivity.

Habitat   In the breeding season, European Goldfinches show a preference for gardens, parks, orchards, and other open woodlands, often near people. At other times of the year, they are commonly found in weedy fields, often where there are tall composites but also in woodlands. In North America they are most commonly found near human habitations.

Behavior   In Europe, they are typically gregarious in the nonbreeding season, and even in the breeding season nonbreeding birds often are found in small flocks. In North America they are most commonly seen at feeders.

Voice   The song is described as a pleasant, liquid *tswitt-witt-witt* or *quilp-ilp-ilp* or a buzzing *zee-zee*. The call is a "grating" *geez* or *tsee-u*.

Similar species   Adults are unmistakable. Juveniles can be confused with young siskins, which have yellow at the sides of the base of the tail, less yellow in the wing, and are much more heavily brown spotted.

Geographic variation   In their range, several subspecies of European Goldfinches have been described. Most birds introduced into North America probably have come from western Europe, where *C. c. britannica* and *C. c. carduelis* occur.

Distribution   *Breeds* in Eurasia, from the British Isles and central Scandinavia east to s Siberia and south to the eastern Atlantic islands, the Mediterranean region, n Africa, the Near East, and Mongolia.
   Winters in southern parts of the breeding range
   Widely introduced into North America. Formerly established in New York but at present not established anywhere. Recently successfully bred in s California (Long Beach). Most or all occasional reports from North America (e.g., from California, Iowa, Illinois, Indiana, Ohio, Wisconsin, Minnesota, Michigan, Ontario) are probably of escaped cage birds. There is a sufficiently large number of such reports that it would seem likely that the European Goldfinch will become established as a breeding species somewhere in North America, perhaps the upper Midwest. As well, there are regular reports from the ne United States and Atlantic Canada that may be vagrants arriving from Europe, although we know of no evidence for this.

Conservation status   At present, we know of no established breeding population of these birds in North America.

Molt   The First Prebasic molt is partial to complete and takes place from August through October. The Definitive Prebasic molt, from mid-July to August is, complete.

Description   Adult males—Red on the face, extending to slightly behind the eye; area around eye and between the bill and eye black; cap and collar black, not extending to the throat; white crescent between red face and black collar; lower side of neck, nape, and mantle cinnamon brown; uppertail coverts whitish; throat and flanks cinnamon brown, brighter than *back* color; midthroat, belly, and undertail coverts white. *Wing* coverts black; primaries, secondaries, and tertials black, with a bright yellow on outer webs (except for the ninth primary), forming a broad yellow band on the wing when spread; wing feathers black posteriorly, with triangular white tips. *Tail* black with white tips on inner rectrices. **Adult females**—Like adult males but with red on face extending only to the back of eye. **Juveniles**—Pale brown with light brown spotting on crown, breast, and belly; mantle grayish olive with faint brown streaks; *wings* like adults' but with buff brown tips to tertials, secondaries, and primaries. *Bill* horn-colored white to cream white, with tip gray to black; *legs* and *feet* pale flesh colored; *iris* dark brown to black.

Hybrids   European Goldfinches have hybridized with a number of other species, including Common Redpolls and Eurasian Siskins, and in captivity with individuals of several other closely related species.

References   Clement et al. (1993), Cramp and Perrins (1994a), Gray (1958).

42.1 European Goldfinch *Carduelis carduelis*, Oxon, UK, December 2003. A medium-size *Carduelis* finch with a relatively long, sharply pointed bill. Distinctive. Red face contrasts with broad white slash across side of head and black crown and half collar. Body mostly cinnamon brown, with white belly. Long, black wings show flashy yellow band on coverts and flight feathers, and white tips to tertials and primaries (George Reszeter).

4 3 **Oriental Greenfinch**

(Carduelis sinica)

Measurements
Length: 12.4–19.0 cm; 5.0–5.5 in.
Wing: 76–85 mm; 3.0–3.3 in. (sexes similar in size).
Mass: 30.8–31.8 g (Alaska).

The Oriental Greenfinch is an Asiatic species that is casual in western Alaska (most records are from mid-May through mid-June).

Habitat   In Asia, Oriental Greenfinches are found in open woodlands, woodland edges, parks and gardens, and rhododendron and coniferous forests.

Behavior   In their normal range, Oriental Greenfinches are found in pairs or small groups, and in winter sometimes in flocks of up to a thousand individuals. They feed principally on seeds but take some insects. In some places (e.g., Japan) they readily come to feeders.

Voice   The song of the Oriental Greenfinch is like that of the Greenfinch (*C. chloris*), but with some harsher notes, *kirr* or *korr*. It has a distinctive twittering flight call, *dzi-dzi-i-dzi-i*.

Similar species   In our area there are no similar species.

Geographic variation   Several different subspecies are recognized. *C. s. kawarahiba*, which breeds on Kamchatka Peninsula, Sakhalin Island, and the Kurile Islands, is the race that wanders to Alaska. Male *C. s. kawarahiba* have a deep green head, face, and throat, a gray moustachial streak, chocolate brown mantle, and a yellowish green rump; females are like the nominate race.

Distribution   *Breeds* from Amurland, Ussuriland, Sakhalin, the Kuril Islands, and Kamchatka south to central and e China, Japan, and the Bonin and Volcano islands.
   Winters in the southern part of the breeding range, casually south to Taiwan.
   Migrates casually through the Aleutian Islands (Attu [May], Buldir [June, August], and Shemya [September]); there is also a record from St. Paul Island, the Pribilof Islands, Alaska, 12–14 June 1996; often found in small flocks. There are about eighteen records since 1976. There is a record of a female, 5 December 1986–3 April 1987, from Arcata, California, which may have been an escaped cage bird.

Conservation status   Extralimital in our area.

Molt   There is a complete Prebasic molt, July through October.

Description   **Adult males**—Forehead, lores, and ear coverts dark olive green to blackish; mantle, upper back, and scapulars cinnamon brown; *rump* paler brown to yellowish toward tail; breast and flanks light cinnamon brown, with yellow belly and undertail coverts; *tail* black, with extensive yellow in the bases of the lateral rectrices; lesser and median coverts olive brown, tinged with bright green; primary coverts black; primaries and secondaries black, with broad yellow bases; secondaries broadly edged pale grayish white. **Adult females**—Like males but duller. *Bill* pale pink or horn colored; *legs* and *feet* pale or pink; *iris* black.

Hybrids   Oriental Greenfinches have been hybridized with European Goldfinches and Himalayan Greenfinches (*C. spinoides*) in captivity.

References   Clement et al. (1993), Dunn et al. (2002), Gray (1958), and Kessel and Gibson (1978).

43.1 Male Oriental Greenfinch *Carduelis sinica*, Japan, March 1999. A large, rather stocky *Carduelis* finch with long wings and a stout, deep-based bill. Brownish overall, with contrasting gray nape and crown and olive green face and forehead. Wings mostly brown, with flashy yellow panel at base of primaries. Blackish tail shows some yellow edging at base. Bill pinkish (Mike Danzenbaker).

43.2 Female Oriental Greenfinch *Carduelis sinica*, Japan, December 1997. Similar to male but duller overall. Head mostly grayish, lacking olive green tones on auriculars. Underparts pale brown, with yellow undertail coverts. Wings with bright yellow bar at base of primaries, contrasting with black primary coverts. Tertials blackish, broadly tipped and edged pale gray. Could be confused with a female Evening Grosbeak but smaller, and note warmer brown body and yellow in wing (Mike Danzenbaker).

44 Eurasian Bullfinch

(Pyrrhula pyrrhula)

Measurements
Length: 14.5–16.0 cm; 5.7–6.3 in.
Wing: 87–97 mm; 3.4–3.8 in. (geographically variable; sexes similar in size).
Mass: 21.0–27.0 g (Britain).

The Eurasian Bullfinch is a Palearctic species that is casual in North America. It is also known as the Bullfinch or Common Bullfinch.

Habitat   In northern Eurasia, Bullfinches breed in coniferous taiga forest as well as in mixed woodlands; in winter they occur in a variety of habitats including scrub, open woodlands, and urban parkland.

Behavior   Bullfinches generally occur singly, in pairs, or, in migration and winter, in small scattered flocks. They are quiet, shy birds. On the ground they move rapidly in short hops.

Voice   The Bullfinch call is a soft, piping *teu* or *phew*. The song is variable, but not loud, and consists of call notes interspersed with other piping and warbling notes.

Similar species   Although there are several bullfinch species in the Old World, no similar bird occurs in North America.

Geographic variation   Several subspecies are found in Eurasia; these differ principally in size and intensity of coloration. *P. p. cassinii*, which breeds on Kamchatka and the northern Kuril Islands, is probably the race that wanders into Alaska; it is similar to the nominate subspecies, but ventrally the females are paler, and dorsally both sexes are paler and purer gray.

Distribution   *Breeds* from the British Isles, n Scandinavia, n Russia, and n Siberia south to s Europe, n Iran, Ussuriland, Sakhalin, Japan, the Kuril Islands, and Kamchatka, and in s Siberia and n Mongolia.
   Winters throughout the breeding range and south to s Europe, central China, Korea, and s Japan.
   Migrates casually in Alaska on St. Lawrence (May and June) and Nunivak (October and November) islands, the w Aleutians (Attu, Agattu [6 June], Shemya [September]), and to the mainland of w and s coastal Alaska (Anik, Anchorage [November]); also reported in se (Petersburg [March]) and central (Nulato [January]) Alaska.

Conservation status   Extralimital in our area, but this is a common bird within its normal range.

Molt   The First Basic plumage is acquired by a partial First Prebasic molt, August through October, that involves head and body feathers, lesser and median upper wing coverts, some of the greater coverts, and usually the tertials. The Definitive Basic plumage is acquired by a complete Prebasic molt that occurs in late August through October.

Description   Adult males—Forehead, lores, and chin black; nape and mantle gray; ear coverts, throat, flanks, and belly deep pink; *rump* white; lower belly and undertail coverts white; *tail* black, *wings* black with gray median coverts and gray-tipped greater coverts, forming a conspicuous single gray wing bar. **Adult females**—Like adult males but gray where males are pink. **First-winter birds** after molt resemble adults, but they retain their Juvenal greater coverts and alulae. **Juveniles** resemble adult females, but the black on the face is replaced with dull brown as are the mantle, back, and scapulars; the median and the tips of the greater coverts are brown. *Bill* of adults is black, and of first-winter birds a dull horn color; *legs* and *feet* dark brown or blackish brown; *iris* black.

Hybrids   Bullfinches have hybridized with a number of other carduelines in captivity.

References   Clement et al. (1993), Cramp and Perrins (1994a), Gray (1958), Kessel and Gibson (1978).

44.1 Male Eurasian Bullfinch *Pyrrhula p. cassini*, Gambell, St. Lawrence Island, Alaska, USA, May 2001. A decidedly plump, medium-size finch with a bull-necked appearance and a thick-based, stubby bill. Highly distinctive with rose pink underparts and cheeks, contrasting with uniform ashy gray mantle and scapulars and black foreface and crown. Wings black, with broad white tips to greater coverts. White rump and undertail coverts (barely visible here) obvious in flight (Phil Davis).

44.2 Male Eurasian Bullfinch *Pyrrhula p. cassini*, Gambell, St. Lawrence Island, Alaska, USA, May 2001. Another view of the same male showing the contrast between the pale gray mantle, black crown and chin, and deep pink cheeks and underparts. The large white rump patch is clearly visible and contrasts strongly with the black wings and tail. There is nothing similar to this spring vagrant to western Alaska (Phil Davis).

44.3 Female Eurasian Bullfinch *Pyrrhula p. pileata*, Oxon, UK, November 2003. Much duller than male, with brownish gray underparts and auriculars. The females of the various forms of Eurasian Bullfinch are all rather similar. The form that occurs as a rare visitor to Alaska is *P. p. cassini*. It differs from the depicted British bird in having paler and grayer mantle and underparts (George Reszeter).

45 Evening Grosbeak

(Coccothraustes vespertinus)

Measurements
Length: 17.5–21.5 cm; 7.0–8.5 in.
Wing: 100–117 mm; 3.9–4.6 in. (males somewhat larger than females).
Mass: Male av. 61.8 g, female av. 61.0 g (Massachusetts); male av. 55.7 g, female av. 54.6 g (Utah).

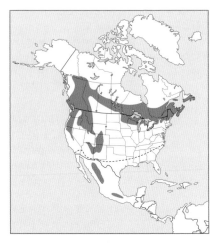

The Evening Grosbeak is a large, stocky finch of the northern coniferous or hardwood forests. These birds are irruptive migrants, and in migration and winter they are usually found in noisy flocks. The massive pale greenish yellow or yellow beak is distinctive. Males are bright yellow below, with a bold yellow supercilium and white secondaries; females have white edges to the secondaries and white at the base of the inner primaries.

Habitat Evening Grosbeaks are found in coniferous and mixed forests; in migration and winter, they are found in a variety of habitats, including urban parks. In the Rocky Mountains, they are common in spruce-fir forests and less common in pine-oak, piñon-juniper, or ponderosa pine and aspen woodlands. In Quebec, they are found mainly in mature and second-growth coniferous woods, especially in spruce-fir woods. On the Upper Peninsula of Michigan, they are found in hardwood forests but move into jack pine woods during budworm outbreaks. In Mexico, they are found in pine or pine-oak woodlands. In the late nineteenth and first half of the twentieth centuries, these finches rapidly expanded their range eastward, perhaps at least in part because of the planting of box elders (Manitoba maples) in cities and windbreaks. These trees produce large numbers of seeds that persist on the trees into winter, providing the grosbeaks with an easily obtained and abundant source of food. Evening Grosbeaks also eat budworms when available, and periodic outbreaks of these insects in the northeastern boreal forest are thought to have encouraged their movement into that region.

Behavior Evening Grosbeaks feed on a variety of buds as well as the seeds of conifers (e.g., ponderosa pine) and the fruits and seeds of a variety of deciduous trees (elm, boxelder and other maples, mountain ash). Their young are fed a variety of insect larvae and fruits. In summer, Evening Grosbeaks are relatively quiet and inconspicuous and can be difficult to find, but in the nonbreeding season, they are nomadic, gregarious, and noisy and aggressive toward other species, often appearing at feeders (where they seem to prefer sunflower seeds). They often feed on salt along roadsides (where many are killed by traffic).

Voice Evening Grosbeaks are most commonly heard as they fly overhead, giving their distinctive, ringing *clear, peer,* or *cle-ip* call. The song is apparently a repetition of this call.

Similar species Within their range, Evening Grosbeaks are unmistakable, although they superficially resemble large American Goldfinches.

Geographic variation Although three subspecies are generally recognized, geographic variation is weak and clinal. *C. v. vespertinus,* which breeds from Alberta eastward, is relatively short billed, with the yellow on the forehead of males relatively broad (extending 7–11 mm from the bill), whereas *P. v. brooksi,* which breeds in the Pacific Northwest south to California and New Mexico, is slightly smaller billed, with the yellow on the forehead of males relatively narrow (3–8 mm). *C. v. montanus,* resident in southeastern Arizona, has a relatively long and narrow bill and relatively little yellow on the forehead (3–8 mm).

Distribution *Breeds* from extreme s Yukon, central and s British Columbia, n Alberta, central Saskatchewan, s Manitoba, central Ontario, and Quebec (north to La Sarre, Lac Saint-Jean, Baie-Trinité, and east to Sept-Îles, Anticosti Island, and the Magdalen Islands) to central Newfoundland and the Maritime Provinces; in the mountains of the west, south to central California, w-central and e Nevada, central and se Arizona, and s New Mexico; and in the Mexican highlands from w Chihuahua to Durango and from Michoacán, México, and Puebla to w-central Veracruz and central Oaxaca (rare and declining); east of the Rockies they are found to sw South Dakota (Black Hills), central and ne Minnesota, n Wisconsin, central Michigan, s Ontario, n New York, and central Massachusetts, casually to n New Jersey. Regular in summer in n British Columbia and s-central and se Yukon, but there are no confirmed breeding records.

Winters throughout the breeding range south, irregularly, to s California, s Arizona, Oaxaca, w and central Texas, the northern portions of the Gulf states, Georgia, and South Carolina, casually south to the Gulf Coast and central Florida.

Casual in e-central, s-central, and se Alaska, s Mackenzie, and on Bermuda. Accidental in the British Isles (St. Kilda, Nethybridge) and Norway (Østfold, Sør-Trøndelag).

Conservation status This is a widespread and locally abundant species. In winter, Evening Grosbeaks are frequently killed by flying into windows near feeders, and, as mentioned above, large numbers are sometimes killed by vehicles as the grosbeaks gather salt and grit along the roads. For example, at least two thousand dead birds were counted along a 16 km stretch of highway in southern British Columbia. Under some circumstances commercial logging may benefit Evening Grosbeaks, as they are more common in thinned stands of Douglas fir than in unthinned stands. Historically, this was principally a western species, but it spread rapidly eastward in the twentieth century. For some reason, however, it is now rapidly declining in the Northeast.

Molt The Prejuvenal molt occurs as the young fledge. The Juvenal plumage is similar to the Definitive Basic plumage. The First Basic plumage is acquired by a partial First Prebasic molt of body feathers and coverts, with Juvenal remiges and rectrices retained. The First Prealternate molt is absent or limited and may include some head and neck feathers. The First Prealternate plumage is similar to the First Prebasic plumage. The Definitive Basic plumage is acquired by a complete Definitive Prebasic molt, which occurs August to November.

Description   Adult males—Forehead, supercilium (to area above the middle of the ear coverts) bright yellow; crown black; feathers at the base of the bill, lores, sides of face, nape, and throat and upper chest dark warm brown, sometimes washed with yellow; *back* becomes more yellow laterally and posteriorily; uppertail coverts black, narrowly edged or tipped with yellow; *tail* black; *underparts* become progressively more yellow from the breast to the undertail coverts, which are yellow; *wings* are black except for the inner greater coverts, innermost secondaries, and tertials, which are white; thighs are black. **Adult females**—Forehead, crown, and upper nape gray to gray brown; lores and feathers at the base of the bill black, sometimes with a hint of a short white stripe above the lores; ear coverts and nape gray, washed with yellow; mantle gray; uppertail coverts black, broadly tipped with white; rectrices black, tipped with white; *underparts* gray, often washed with yellow, especially on the flanks; undertail coverts buffy white; all *wing* feathers black except the median and outer greater coverts; inner greater coverts are white; all but the outermost primaries have white bases; the outer webs of the inner secondaries and tertials are white, variably washed with gray; thighs black. **Juveniles** resemble adult females prior to the First Basic molt but are duller. *Bill* is off-white in the nonbreeding season, becoming greenish yellow or yellow by late spring; *legs* and *feet* dull pink to brown, occasionally washed with gray or brown gray at tarsus; *iris* dark brown.

Hybrids   No hybrids have been reported.

References   Cramp and Perrins (1994a), Gillihan and Byers (2001), Howell and Webb (1995), Pyle (1997).

45.1 Male Evening Grosbeak *Coccothraustes v. vespertinus*, Orono, Ontario, Canada, February 1985. A hefty, short-tailed, and large-headed finch with massive, deep-based bill. Dark brown on upper back, head, and throat, blending to yellow on lower back and remaining underparts. Bright yellow stripe defining forehead and short supercilium stands out. Wings black, with striking white panel on tertials and secondaries. Large bill pinkish yellow (James Richards).

45.2 Male Evening Grosbeak *Coccothraustes v. vespertinus*, Algonquin Provincial Park, Ontario, Canada, February 2002. In this front view notice the contrast between the blackish brown head and the bright yellow supercilium and massive, chalky white bill. The yellow underparts are sullied with brown on the belly (Sam Barone).

45.3 Female Evening Grosbeak *Coccothraustes v. vespertinus*, Orono, Ontario, Canada, February 1990. Mostly pale gray, slightly darker on head, with contrasting yellow olive collar, sides of breast, and flanks. Wings mosly black, with complex pattern of white on greater coverts, secondaries, and at base of primaries. Nothing similar within its range (James Richards).

45.4 Male Evening Grosbeak *Coccothraustes v. brooksi*, Glacier National Park, Montana, USA, June 2001. Birds from western populations are, on average, slightly longer billed than those from the East. Plumage similar to that of eastern birds, though yellow on forehead slightly reduced. As on eastern birds, note the striking black and white wing pattern and deep brown and yellow body plumage (Brian E. Small).

45.5 Adult female Evening Grosbeak *Coccothraustes v. brooksi*, Glacier National Park, Montana, USA, June 2001. Apart from slightly longer bill, similar to eastern female. Note the rather complex wing pattern, with gray and white edges to greater coverts, tertials, and secondaries and some white at the base of the primaries. Undertail coverts white. Uppertail coverts black, with large white tips (Brian E. Small).

45.6 Juvenal male Evening Grosbeak *Coccothraustes v. brooksii*, Estes Park, Colorado, USA, June 2001. Like a dingy version of adult male, with reduced and paler brown wash on head and mantle and largely off-white underparts. Some yellow is present on the supercilium and sides of breast. Wings mostly black, with obvious off-white panel on tertials. Unlike adult's, the bill is mostly dusky, with pinkish base to lower mandible (Rick and Nora Bowers).

46 Hawfinch

(Coccothraustes coccothraustes)

Measurements
Length: 16.0–18.0 cm; 6.3–7.1 in.
Wing: 97–110 mm; 3.8–4.3 in. (Europe).
Mass: 44.5–54.8 g (*C. c. japonicus*).

The Hawfinch is extralimital in our area, but it wanders casually to western Alaska, where in recent years it has been recorded almost annually.

Habitat   Hawfinches occur in old deciduous or mixed forests, parkland, scrub, and bushy areas.

Behavior   In their normal range, Hawfinches are usually found in pairs or small groups. They are shy or wary birds, generally seen feeding quietly in trees or on the ground under trees. Their flight is undulating, and on the ground they walk with an upright stance. In some parts of Europe they are a common species in city parks, and they regularly come to feeders.

Voice   The call is described as a soft, piping *teu* or *deu* or *deu deu*. The song is apparently simply the call repeated several times, a piping warble.

Similar species   Hawfinches resemble Evening Grosbeaks, but their ranges do not overlap at all.

Geographic variation   Several subspecies of Hawfinches occur in Eurasia. *C. c. japonicus*, which breeds on Sakhalin Island and on central and southern Kamchatka south to northern Japan, is the race that probably wanders to Alaska. *C. c. japonicus* is smaller and paler than the nominate subspecies (which breeds in northern Europe) and has more white on the belly and less on the tip of the tail.

Distribution   *Breeds* in Eurasia, from the British Isles, s Scandinavia, central Russia, and central Siberia south to nw Africa, the Mediterranean region, Asia Minor, n Iran, Amurland, Manchuria, Sakhalin, and Japan.
   Winters throughout the breeding range south to n Africa, s Iran, nw India, n China, and the Ryukyu, Bonin, and Volcano islands.
   Casual spring migrant (late May and June) in the w and central Aleutian Islands (from Attu and Adak to Shemya [May]) and the Pribilofs (November; June), on St. Matthew Island (one May record) and St. Lawrence Island, and in w Alaska (Noatak River, Dillingham).

Conservation status   Extralimital in our area.

Molt   The First Basic plumage is acquired by a partial First Prebasic molt, during which the Juvenal greater coverts and alulae are retained; this molt takes place in August and September. The Definitive Basic plumage is acquired by a complete Basic molt in late July through September.

Description   Adult males—Lower forehead (at base of bill), lores, and chin and up-per throat black; ear coverts and cheeks warm cinnamon or orangish; crown warm brown or cinnamon; nape and sides of neck gray; mantle rich chocolate brown; lower back, rump, and uppertail coverts cinnamon brown; *tail* cinnamon brown with black lateral rectrices and a white tip; breast, flanks, and belly light pinkish brown; undertail coverts whitish to grayish white; lesser coverts blackish; median coverts white or pale buffy white, forming a wing bar on the folded wing; remiges black, with a bluish tinge to the secondaries and the midinner webs of the primaries white, forming a wing stripe that is visible in flight. **Adult females**—Very much like adult males but duller in color, especially on the head. **First winter**—Males resemble adults but have deep blue secondaries and a thin dark line around the base of the bill; females are like first-winter males but paler in color. **Juveniles** resemble adults but have brown mottling on their breast. ***Bill*** of adults dark, and of first-winter birds yellowish to brown; *legs* and *feet* pale pinkish brown; *iris* dark brown.

Hybrids   There is a doubtful record of a hybrid Hawfinch and Eurasian Bullfinch, and in captivity Hawfinches have been hybridized with Greenfinches (*Carduelis chloris*).

References   Clement et al. (1993), Cramp and Perrins (1994a), Gray (1958), and Kessel and Gibson (1978).

46.1 Male Hawfinch *Coccothraustes coccothraustes*, Japan, May 1998. A hefty, short-tailed, and large-headed finch with a massive, deep-based bill. Predominately pinkish brown, darker on mantle, and with cinnamon brown crown and auriculars. Powerful, steel gray bill offset by small black mask and bib. Wings bluish black, with white slash on greater coverts. Tail with large white spots at tip (Mike Danzenbaker).

46.2 Adult female Hawfinch *Coccothraustes coccothraustes*, Kent, UK, June 1991. Similar to male but duller overall, appearing slightly washed out. Differs mostly in showing pale gray edges to secondary feathers, forming an obvious panel on closed wing (George Reszeter)

Appendix

Type	Typical	Variants		
1				
2				
3				
4				
5				
6				
7				
8		no others recorded		

250 msec

Red Crossbill call types. From Adkisson (1996), used with permission.

Glossary

Alternate plumage. The plumage that replaces the Basic plumage. Some finches lack an Alternate plumage.

Alula. A small feather attached to the first digit, at the bend of the wing. The plural is alulae.

Auriculars. The ear coverts.

Basic plumage. The plumage that replaces either the Juvenal plumage or the Alternate plumage. The First Basic plumage (or Basic I plumage) replaces the Juvenal plumage. Most tanagers and cardinals have a distinctive first basic plumage. Finches generally do not have a distinct Alternate plumage; the First Basic plumage is like later Basic plumages or only little different; these later plumages are called the Definitive Basic plumage.

Braces. Pale parallel streaks on the back, like "suspenders."

Conspecific. The same species.

Coverts. Feathers that cover the bases on the primaries (primary coverts) or secondaries (usually called lesser, median, and greater coverts but sometimes greater secondary coverts, etc.); there are also underwing coverts (feathers on the underside of the wing, near to the body) and undertail coverts.

Culmen. The upper mandible or bill.

Family. A taxonomic category containing one to several genera. The tanagers, cardinals, and finches are often put in the families Thraupidae, Cardinalidae, and Fringillidae, respectively. In zoological nomenclature, all families end in the suffix -idae.

Genus. A subdivision of the family, containing one to several species. A genus containing only one species is called a monotypic genus. The plural is genera.

Juvenal plumage. The plumage that replaces the natal down; the Juvenal plumage is acquired while the young bird is in the nest, perhaps completed shortly after it leaves the nest.

Juvenile. In sparrows, a juvenile is a bird in Juvenal plumage. More generally, juvenile can be used to refer to any subadult bird, that is, a bird that cannot yet breed. All the species discussed in this book, however, potentially reach reproductive maturity in the spring following their birth.

Lores. The area between the eye and the upper mandible.

Malar stripe. The area on the side of the throat immediately below the base of the lower mandible.

Mandible. Strictly, the mandible is the bone (several fused bones) of the lower jaw and its horny covering, and in this sense is contrasted with maxilla. More generally, however, the term refers to the bill, with upper mandible (or culmen) and lower mandible being commonly used.

Monotypic. A species with no named subspecies; only member of its group (e.g. only species in a genus).

Moustachial stripe. A stripe on some birds running back from the base of the bill.

Nominate subspecies (race). The subspecies whose subspecific name is the same as the species name, e.g., *Carpodacus purpureus purpureus* (the nominate subspecies), as opposed to *Carpodacus purpureus californicus* (a different subspecies).

Prealternate molt. This is the molt during which birds acquire their Alternate plumage. In many species this is incomplete, that is to say, not all of the Basic plumage is replaced, and in others this molt does not occur. In species in which it is possible to differentiate between birds in their First Alternate plumage and subsequent Alternate plumages (Definitive Alternate plumages), we often differentiate between the First Prealternate and the Definitive Prealternate molts.

Prebasic molt. This is the molt during which birds acquire their Basic plumage. Particularly in first-year birds, this molt may be incomplete, that is to say, not all of the Juvenal or Alternate plumage is replaced. In species in which it is possible to differentiate between birds in their First Basic plumage and those in subsequent Basic plumages (Definitive Basic plumages), we often differentiate between the First Prebasic and the Definitive Prebasic molts.

Presupplemental molt. In some species there is an extra molt of some of the body feathers, and occasionally of some of the coverts, that occurs before the First Prebasic molt. This has been called a Presupplemental molt.

Rectrices. Tail feathers (not including coverts).

Remiges. Primary and secondary wing feathers.

Scapulars. Feathers covering the shoulders.

Species. Variously defined, but commonly as "groups of interbreeding populations that are reproductively isolated from other such groups." Generally, individuals from different species do not interbreed and produce viable, fertile offspring. If this occurs only occasionally, or is geographically restricted, the two groups are considered to be effectively reproductively isolated and may be treated as two different species. For example, Rose-breasted and Black-headed grosbeaks interbreed occasionally in the Great Plains but are now considered to be two different species because in areas where both species occur most individuals are not hybrids.

Submoustachial stripe. A stripe between the moustachial and malar stripes.

Subspecies. A geographically and morphologically defined population (or group of populations) of one species.

Supercilium. The stripe that runs above the eye.

Tomium (tomial). The cutting edge of the mandible.

Truncate. Broad and perhaps shortened. Many songbirds that retain their outer primaries during the First Prebasic molt can be aged by the shape of their outer rectrices, which are narrower in young birds and broader and more truncate in adults. Also, the shape of the outer primaries can be used in aging some species (those with incomplete First Prebasic molts) because the retained Juvenal primaries are narrower and more tapered than those of adults.

References

Adkisson, C. S. 1977. Morphological variation in North American Pine Grosbeaks. *Wilson Bulletin* 89:380–395

Adkisson, C. S. 1996. Red Crossbill (*Loxia curvirostra*). In *The Birds of North America*, No. 256 (A. Poole and F. Gill, eds.). The Birds of North America, Inc., Philadelphia, PA

Adkisson, C. S. 1999. Pine Grosbeak (*Pinicola enucleator*). In *The Birds of North America*, No. 456 (A. Poole and F. Gill, eds.). The Birds of North America, Inc., Philadelphia, PA

Alcorn, J. R. 1988. *The Birds of Nevada*. Fairview West Publ., Fallon, NV

American Ornithologists' Union. 1957. *Check-list of North American Birds*, 5th edition. American Ornithologists' Union, Baltimore, MD

American Ornithologists' Union. 1998. *Check-list of North American Birds*, 7th edition. American Ornithologists' Union, Washington, DC

Austin, O. L., Jr. (ed.). *Life Histories of North American Cardinals, Buntings, Towhees, Finches, Sparrows, and Allies*. Bull. 237, U.S. Nat. Mus., Parts 2 and 3; Bull. 237, U.S. Nat. Mus, Parts 2 and 3, Smithsonian Inst., Washington, DC

Beadle, D., and B. Henshaw. 1996. Identification of "Greenland" and Common Redpoll *Carduelis flammea rostrata*. *Birder's Journal* 5:44–47

Beaton, G., P. W. Sykes, Jr., and J. W. Parrish, Jr. 2003. *Annotated Checklist of Georgia Birds*. Occ. Publ. No. 14., Georgia Ornithol. Soc., Atlanta, GA

Benkman, C. W. 1992. White-winged Crossbill (*Loxia leucoptera*). In *The Birds of North America*, No. 27 (A. Poole, P. Stettenheim, and F. Gill, eds.). The Birds of North America, Inc., Philadelphia, PA

Benkman, C. W. 1993. Adaptation to single resources and the evolution of crossbills (*Loxia*) diversity. *Ecology Monographs* 63:305–325

Busby, W. H., and J. L. Zimmerman. 2001. *Kansas Breeding Bird Atlas*. Univ. Press of Kansas, Lawrence, KS

Campbell, R. W., N. K. Dawe, I. McTaggart-Cowan, J. M. Cooper, G. W. Kaiser, A. C. Stewart, and M.C.E. McNall. 2001. *The Birds of British Columbia*, Vol. 4. UBC Press, Vancouver, BC

Christie, D. S., B. E. Dalzell, M. David, R. Doiron, D. G. Gibson, M. H. Lushington, P. A. Pearce, S. I. Tingley, and J. G. Watson. 2004. *Birds of New Brunswick: An Annotated List*. The New Brunswick Museum, Monograph Series (Natural Science) No. 10, St. John, NB

Clement, P., A. Harris, and J. Davis. 1993. *Finches & Sparrows: An Identification Guide*. A. & C. Black, London, UK

Cramp, S., and C. M. Perrins (eds.). 1994a. *Handbook of the Birds of Europe, the Middle East, and North Africa*, Vol. 8. Oxford Univ. Press, Oxford, UK

Cramp, S., and C. M. Perrins (eds.). 1994b. *Handbook of the Birds of Europe, the Middle East, and North Africa*, Vol. 9. Oxford Univ. Press, Oxford, UK

Curson, J., D. Quinn, and D. Beadle. 1994. *Warblers of the Americas: An Identification Guide*. Houghton Mifflin Co., Boston, MA

Cyr, A., and J. Larivée. 1995. *Atlas saisonnier des oiseaux du Québec*. Presses de l'Université de Sherbrooke et Société de Loisir Ornithologique de l'Estrie, Sherbrooke, PQ

Dau, C. P., and D. D. Gibson. 1974. Common Rose Finch, a first record for North America. *Auk* 91:185–186

Davis, J. N. 1999. Lawrence's Goldfinch (*Carduelis lawrencei*). In *The Birds of North America*, No. 480 (A. Poole and F. Gill, eds.). The Birds of North America, Inc., Philadelphia, PA

Dawson, W. R. 1997. Pine Siskin (*Carduelis pinus*). In *The Birds of North America*, No. 280 (A. Poole and F. Gill, eds.). The Birds of North America, Inc., Philadelphia, PA

Dudley, S., T. Benton, P. Fraser, and J. Ryan. 1996. *Rare Birds Day by Day*. T. & A. D. Poyser, London, UK

Dunn, J. L., and K. L. Garrett. 1997. *A Field Guide to the Warblers of North America*. Houghton Mifflin Co., Boston, MA

Dunn, J. L., D. L. Dittmann, K. L. Garrett, G. Lasley, M. B. Robbins, C. Sexton, S. Tingley, and T. Tobish. 2002. *ABA Checklist: Birds of the Continental United States and Canada*. American Birding Assoc., Inc., Colorado Springs, CO

Dunning, Jr., J. B. 1993. *CRC Handbook of Avian Body Masses*. CRC Press, Boca Raton, FL

Eddleman, W. R. 2002. Hepatic Tanager (*Piranga flava*). In *The Birds of North America*, No. 655 (A. Poole and F. Gill, eds.). The Birds of North America, Inc., Philadelphia, PA

Flint, V. E., R. L. Boehme, Y. V. Kostin, and A. A. Kuznetsov. 1984. *A Field Guide to Birds of the USSR*. Princeton Univ. Press, Princeton, NJ

Garrido, O. H., K. C. Parkes, G. B. Reynard, A. Kirkconnell, and R. Sutton. 1997. Taxonomy of the Stripe-headed Tanager, genus *Spindalis* (Aves: Thraupidae) of the West Indies. *Wilson Bulletin* 109:561–594

Gauthier, J., and Y. Aubry (eds.). 1996. *The Breeding Birds of Québec: Atlas of the Breeding Birds of Southern Québec*. Assn. québécoise des groupes d'ornithologues, Prov. of Quebec Soc. for the Protection of Birds, Canadian Wildlife Service, Environment Canada, Québec Region, Montréal, PQ

Gillihan, S. W., and B. Byers. 2001. Evening Grosbeak (*Coccothraustes vespertinus*). In *The Birds of North America*, No. 599 (A. Poole and F. Gill, eds.). The Birds of North America, Inc., Philadelphia, PA

Godfrey, W. E. 1986. *The Birds of Canada*. Nat. Mus. Canada, Ottawa, ON

Gray, A. P. 1958. *Bird Hybrids*. Commonwealth Agricultural Bureaux, Farnham Royal, Bucks, UK

Green, E., V. R. Muehter, and W. Davison. 1996. Lazuli Bunting (*Passerina amoena*). In *The Birds of North America*, No. 232 (A. Poole and F. Gill, eds.). The Birds of North America, Inc., Philadelphia, PA

Groschupf, K. D., and C. W. Thompson. 1998. Varied Bunting (*Passerina versicolor*). In *The Birds of North America*, No. 351 (A. Poole and F. Gill, eds.). The Birds of North America, Inc., Philadelphia, PA

Groth, J. G. 1988. Resolution of cryptic species in Appalachian Red Crossbills. *Condor* 90:745–760

Groth, J. G. 1993a. Evolutionary differentiation in morphology, vocalizations, and allozymes among nomadic sibling species in the North American Red Crossbill (*Loxia curvirostra*) complex. *Univ. California Publs. Zool.* 127:1–143

Groth, J. G. 1993b. Call matching and positive assortative mating in Red Crossbills. *Auk* 110:398–401

Hahn, T. P. 1996. Cassin's Finch (*Carpodacus cassinii*). In *The Birds of North America*, No. 240 (A. Poole and F. Gill, eds.). The Birds of North America, Inc., Philadelphia, PA

Halkin, S. L., and S. U. Linville. 1999. Northern Cardinal (*Cardinalis cardinalis*). In *The Birds of North America*, No. 440 (A. Poole and F. Gill, eds.). The Birds of North America, Inc., Philadelphia, PA

Hill, G. E. 1993. House Finch (*Carpodacus mexicanus*). In *The Birds of North America*, No. 46 (A. Poole and F. Gill, eds.). The Birds of North America, Inc., Philadelphia, PA

Hill, G. E. 1995. Black-headed Grosbeak (*Pheucticus melanocephalus*). In *The Birds of North America*, No. 143 (A. Poole and F. Gill, eds.). The Birds of North America, Inc., Philadelphia, PA

Howell, S.N.G., and S. Webb. 1995. *A Guide to the Birds of Mexico and Northern Central America*. Oxford Univ. Press, Oxford, UK

Hudon, J. 1999. Western Tanager (*Piranga ludoviciana*). In *The Birds of North America*, No. 432 (A. Poole and F. Gill, eds.). The Birds of North America, Inc., Philadelphia, PA

Humphrey, P. S., and K. C. Parkes. 1959. An approach to the study of molts and plumages. *Auk* 76:1–31

Ingold, J. L . 1993. Blue Grosbeak (*Guiraca caerulea*). In *The Birds of North America*, No. 79 (A. Poole and F. Gill, eds.). The Birds of North America, Inc., Philadelphia, PA

Isler, M. L., and P. R. Isler. 1987. *The Tanagers*. Smithsonian Inst. Press, Washington, DC

Jaramillo, A., and P. Burke. 1999. *New World Blackbirds: The Icterids*. Princeton Univ. Press, Princeton, NJ

Jehl, J. R., Jr. 2004. *Birdlife of the Churchill Region: Status, History, Biology*. Churchill Northern Studies Centre, Churchill, MB

Johnson, R. E. 1977. Seasonal variation in the Genus *Leucosticte*. *Condor* 79:76–86

Johnson, R. E. 2002. Black Rosy-Finch (*Leucosticte atrata*). In *The Birds of North America*, No. 678 (A. Poole and F. Gill, eds.). The Birds of North America, Inc., Philadelphia, PA

Johnson, R. E., P. Hendricks, D. L. Pattie, and K. B. Hunter. 2000. Brown-capped Rosy-Finch (*Leucosticte australis*). In *The Birds of North America,* No. 536 (A. Poole and F. Gill, eds.). The Birds of North America, Inc., Philadelphia, PA

Jones, H. L. 2003. *Birds of Belize*. Univ. Texas Press, Austin, TX

Kaufman, K. 1990. *Advanced Birding*. Houghton Mifflin Co., Boston, MA

Kessel, B., and D. D. Gibson. 1978. *Status and Distribution of Alaska Birds*. Studies in Avian Biology No. 1, Cooper Ornithol. Soc., Lawrence, KS

Kingery, H. E. (ed.). 1998. *Colorado Breeding Bird Atlas*. Colorado Wildlife Heritage Foundation, Denver, CO

Knox, A. G., and P. E. Lowther. 2000a. Common Redpoll (*Carduelis flammea*). In *The Birds of North America*, No. 543 (A. Poole and F. Gill, eds.). The Birds of North America, Inc., Philadelphia, PA

Knox, A. G., and P. E. Lowther. 2000b. Hoary Redpoll (*Carduelis hornemanni*). In *The Birds of North America*, No. 544 (A. Poole and F. Gill, eds.). The Birds of North America, Inc., Philadelphia, PA

Levine, E. (ed.). 1998. *Bull's Birds of New York*. Comstock Publ. Assoc., Ithaca, NY

Lockwood, M. W., and B. Freeman. 2004. *The Texas Ornithological Society Handbook of Texas Birds*. Texas A & M Press, College Station, TX

Lowther, P. E., S. M. Lanyon, and C. W. Thompson. 1999. Painted Bunting (*Passerina ciris*). In *The Birds of North America*, No. 398 (A. Poole and F. Gill, eds.). The Birds of North America, Inc., Philadelphia, PA

MacDougall-Shackleton, S. A., R. E. Johnson, and T. P. Hahn. 2000. Gray-crowned Rosy-Finch (*Leucosticte tephrocotis*). In *The Birds of North America*, No. 559 (A. Poole and F. Gill, eds.). The Birds of North America, Inc., Philadelphia, PA

Marshall, D. B., M. G. Hunter, and A. L. Contreras (eds.). 2003. *Birds of Oregon*. Oregon State Univ. Press, Corvallis, OR

Middleton, A.L.A. 1993. American Goldfinch (*Carduelis tristis*). In *The Birds of North America*, No. 80 (A. Poole and F. Gill, eds.). The Birds of North America, Inc., Philadelphia, PA

Morlan, J. 1991. Identification of female Rose-breasted and Black-headed Grosbeaks. *Birding* 23:220–223

Mowbray, T. B. 1999. Scarlet Tanager (*Piranga olivacea*). In *The Birds of North America*, No. 479 (A. Poole and F. Gill, eds.). The Birds of North America, Inc., Philadelphia, PA

Newton, I. 1973. *Finches*. Taplinger Publ. Co., New York, NY

North American Birds. 2003. Spring migration: March through May 2003. *North American Birds* 57:429

Oberholser, H. C. 1974. *The Bird Life of Texas*, Vol. 2. Univ. Texas Press, Austin, TX

Payne, R. B. 1992. Indigo Bunting (*Passerina cyanea*). In *The Birds of North America*, No. 4 (A. Poole and F. Gill, eds.). The Birds of North America, Inc., Philadelphia, PA

Paynter, R. A., Jr. 1968. *Check-List of Birds of the World*, Vol. 14. Mus. Comparative Zoology, Cambridge, MA

Paynter, R. A., Jr. 1970. *Check-List of Birds of the World*, Vol. 13. Mus. Comparative Zoology, Cambridge, MA

Peterson, W. R., and W. R. Meservey. 2003. *Massachusetts Breeding Bird Atlas*. Massachusetts Audubon Soc., Amherst, MA

Phillips, A., J. Marshall, and G. Monson. 1964. *The Birds of Arizona*. Univ. Arizona Press, Tucson, AZ

Pinel, H. W., W. W. Smith, and C. R. Wershler. 1993. *Alberta Birds, 1971–1980*, Vol. 2, *Passerines*. Nat. Hist. Occ. Paper No. 20, Prov. Mus. Alberta, Edmonton, AB

Pyle, P. 1997. *Identification Guide to North American Birds*, Part 1. Slate Creek Press, Bolinas, CA

Raffaele, H., J. Wiley, O. Garrido, A. Keith, and J. Raffaele. 1998. *A Guide to the Birds of the West Indies*. Princeton Univ. Press, Princeton, NJ

Riddington, R., and S. Volker. 1997. Redpolls from Greenland and Iceland. *Birding World* 10:147–149

Ridgway, R. 1901. *The Birds of North and Middle America*, Part 1. Bull. 50, U.S. Nat. Mus., Smithsonian Inst., Washington, DC

Ridgway, R. 1902. *The Birds of North and Middle America*, Part 2. Bull. 50, U.S. Nat. Mus., Smithsonian Inst., Washington, DC

Rising, J. D. 1983. The Great Plains hybrid zones. *Current Ornithology* 1:131–157

Rising, J. D. 2002. Answers to the June Photo Quiz. *Birding* 34:334–336

Robbins, C. S., D. Bystrak, and P. H. Geissler. 1986. *The Breeding Bird Survey: Its First Fifteen Years, 1965–1979.* U.S. Dept. Interior, Fish and Wildlife Service, Washington, DC

Robertson, W. B., Jr., and G. E. Woolfenden. 1992. *Florida Bird Species: An Annotated List.* Special Publ. No. 6, Florida Ornithological Society, Gainesville, FL

Robinson, W. D. 1996. Summer Tanager (*Piranga rubra*). In *The Birds of North America*, No. 248 (A. Poole and F. Gill, eds.). The Birds of North America, Inc., Philadelphia, PA

Russell, S. M., and G. Monson. 1998. *The Birds of Sonora.* Univ. Arizona Press, Tucson, AZ

Semenchuk, G. P. (ed.). 1992. *The Atlas of the Breeding Birds of Alberta.* Fed. Alberta Naturalists, Edmonton, AB

Seutin, G., P. T. Boag, and L. M. Ratcliffe. 1992. Plumage variability in redpolls from Churchill, Manitoba. *Auk* 109:771–785

Sibley, D. A. 2000. *The Sibley Guide to Birds.* Alfred A. Knopf, New York, NY

Sibley, D. A. 2003. *The Sibley Field Guide to Birds of Eastern North America.* A. A. Knopf, New York, NY

Sinclair, P. H., et al. 2003. *Birds of the Yukon Territory.* UBC Press, Vancouver, BC

Skutch, A. F. 1954. *Life Histories of Central American Birds.* Pacific Coast Avifauna No. 31, Berkeley, CA

Small, A. 1994. *California Birds: Their Status and Distribution.* Ibis Publ. Co., Vista, CA

Stevenson, H. M., and B. H. Anderson. 1994. *The Birdlife of Florida.* Univ. Press of Florida, Gainesville, FL

Taylor, P. (ed.). 2003. *The Birds of Manitoba.* Manitoba Naturalists Soc., Winnipeg, MB

Temple, S. A. 2002. Dickcissel (*Spiza americana*). In *The Birds of North America*, No. 703 (A. Poole and F. Gill, eds.). The Birds of North America, Inc., Philadelphia, PA

Thompson, C. W. 1991a. The sequence of molts and plumages in Painted Buntings and implications for theories of delayed plumage maturation. *Condor* 93:209–235

Thompson, C. W. 1991b. Is the Painted Bunting actually two species? Problems determining species limits between allopatric populations. *Condor* 93:987–1000

Troy, D. M. 1985. A phenetic analysis of the redpolls *Carduelis flammea flammea* and *C. hornemanni exilipes. Auk* 102:82–96

Tweit, R. C., and C. W. Thompson. 1999. Pyrrhuloxia (*Cardinalis sinuatus*). In *The Birds of North America*, No. 391 (A. Poole and F. Gill, eds.). The Birds of North America, Inc., Philadelphia, PA

Udvardy, M.D.F. 1977. *The Audubon Society Field Guide to North American Birds: Western Region.* Alfred A. Knopf, New York, NY

Veit, R. R., and W. R. Peterson. 1993. *Birds of Massachusetts.* Massachusetts Audubon Soc., Lincoln, MA

Watt, D. J., and E. J. Willoughby. 1999. Lesser Goldfinch (*Carduelis tristis*). In *The Birds of North America*, No. 392 (A. Poole and F. Gill, eds.). The Birds of North America, Inc., Philadelphia, PA

Wetmore, A., R. F. Pasquier, and S. L. Olson. 1984. *The Birds of the Republic of Panamá.*

Part 4. Passeriformes: Hirundidnidae (Swallows) to Fringillidae (Finches). Smithsonian Institution Press, Washington, DC

Winker, K., D. D. Gibson, A. L. Sowls, B. E. Lawhead, P. D. Martin, E. P. Hoberg, and D. Causey. 2003. The Birds of St. Matthew Island, Bering Sea. *Wilson Bull.* 114:491–509

Wootton, J. T. 1996. Purple Finch (*Carpodacus purpureus*). In *The Birds of North America*, No. 208 (A. Poole and F. Gill, eds.). The Birds of North America, Inc., Philadelphia, PA

Wyatt, V. E., and C. M. Francis. 2002. Rose-breasted Grosbeak (*Pueucticus ludovicianus*). In *The Birds of North America*, No. 692 (A. Poole and F. Gill, eds.). The Birds of North America, Inc., Philadelphia, PA.

Index

Note 1: The main text section on each species is given in **bold**.
Note 2: Latin genus and species names are abbreviated to the first initial where subentries occur.